WOMEN OF GRACE

Women Healers and Healing Practices

by

Carol Kronwitter

D & S Publications, Inc.

~Speaking Our Truth~

D & S Publications, Inc. is committed to the publication of significant works that in some way move us forward on our life's journey.
For a product catalogue of books and art work contact us at 715-545-8312.

First Edition July, 2001

Artwork by Carol Kronwitter
Editor Mary Jean Porter
Layout by Jackie Pavlow, Northern Images

D & S Publications, Inc.
3073 Hwy. K East
Conover, WI 54519
715-545-8312

DEDICATION

Grace ~
the divine influence
acting within one's heart

This book is dedicated to all
women of grace ~ past, present,
future; to those who heal with
their hands, their hearts,
their voices and their visions.

May we all remember who we are
and to practice what we know.

The material in this book is for informational
purposes only. It is not to be used for diagnosis,
or as a prescription, or to replace
the services of a physician

Acknowledgements

Many blessings to all who made this book possible:

These 20 Women of Grace,

Longtime friend, writing teacher and editor,
Mary Jean Porter,

Publisher, Jeannine Doyle,

Friend and supporter, Juanita,

Spirit sisters and brother.

TABLE OF CONTENTS

Part Three: Bodyworkers

Part Four: Shamans and Spiritual Healers

Part Five: Clairvoyant Healers

Part Six: Animal Healers

THE HEALER'S PRAYER

by Soltahr

Wherever I go, may there be healing,
Whatever my hands touch, may it be healed.
When my mouth utters words,
may they be words of comfort, soothing
and strength.
When my lips are open in song,
may each note, each phrase touch the heart
and memory with warmth and love.
If it be but a smile, or a glance
into the eyes of pain,
may that pain be lessened ~
if only for a moment.
With each beat of my heart,
with each tear that I cry,
with each breath I breathe,
may I too, be healed ~
that I may be a stronger, deeper well
for the energies and powers of health,
wholeness, life and love.
Blessed Be.

INTRODUCTION

Coming of Age

It is 2001. This book is finally in print, eight years after I began it. The timing couldn't be more perfect.

Now, more than at any time in Earth's history, there is an increase in the light or information that is coming to us. Windows to our beings are opening so this information can enter and guide us in all areas of our lives.

If alternative healing practices have served or partially served you, they now can take you to higher levels of healing. How does this work?

Imagine that your brain is like a computer, filled with files of information and programs that determine how you think and feel. These records include genetics, life experiences, beliefs, soul and karmic designs, and personality.

Sometimes these records get in the way. They keep us from holding the results of our meditations, for example. They leave our prayers or intentions only partially realized, or prevent us from receiving the full benefits of a healing program. In other words, we get some but not all; we get better but not completely well.

With the increase of light or information now coming in, our innate wisdom can override the blocks or lines of resistance that keep us from being whole. The process of healing and wholeness then can be simplified and quickened.

This means hope. Hope that we can overcome our diseases and distracting behavior patterns; hope that we can hold the calm and joy of oneness; hope that we can heal the world.

The healing methods outlined in "Women of Grace: Women Healers and Healing Practices" are the foundation for this new way of being. As more information comes into our computers – our beings – our ability to heal and to be healed can expand beyond our imaginings.

We have come of age. We have come home.

The Journey

"Women of Grace: Women Healers and Healing Practices" is a collection of stories about women healers and alternative healing practices in Colorado, New Mexico and Arizona. Although these women live and practice their healing arts in the Southwest, what they do is universal.

"Women of Grace" began with stories about the women in Colorado who have helped me to heal. They and the other women I have met on my journey are as committed to healing themselves as they are to healing others. They are women who practice and teach spirituality.

Some of these women practice methods rooted in Hispanic and Native American traditions, while others use more contemporary nutritional and herbal therapies. Some are psychics, some are bodyworkers. They are all different, yet they are the same: All are guided by their inner wisdom and strong sense of purpose to heal the planet and its people. And in many cases, their stories are my story. They may be your story, too.

My purpose in sharing these stories is to inform the public about the myriad of possibilities that exist today for healing one's body, mind and spirit. As a healer, I have access to a wide network of female and male practitioners of holistic health care. But for those of you who don't, who are just beginning to look for alternatives to Western medicine, may this serve as a guide and a resource.

This book is about women because I believe that women, with their gentle, nurturing and intuitive ways, are natural healers. They are the caregivers, the mothers, the wisdom keepers. And I believe that it is through women – and men who honor the female aspects of themselves – that Earth and her people will heal.

15

The stories began in October 1993 in my hometown of Pueblo, Colorado, and concluded in February 1997. They convey personal aspects of the women's lives and the nature of their work. Some of the women were born into their arts; most of them had awakenings that put them on their paths. Several of the women have moved to other states or countries since the time of their interviews, and many of them have expanded their work to include other elements. Some of these changes, as of March 2000, and where to contact the women follow their stories.

These 20 women are a small representation of the growing number of healers throughout the United States. There is a saying among healers (and in other professions): If you're good, you don't have to advertise. These women, and others like them, don't advertise. People find them and pass their names on. If you have a deep commitment to be healthy, you will find a healer or healers who will guide you. Trust your inner wisdom, trust your higher power. And may your journey be as exciting and inspiring as mine has been and continues to be.

Blessings,
Carol Kronwitter

PART ONE

ALTERNATIVE DOCTORS

Barbara Shears
Doctor of Naturopathy

Natural healing programs aren't easy — they're a major commitment. It's so easy in this culture to take drugs, to fix it. There is no miracle cure from drugs or supplements.

It was a cold, blustery November day in Colorado Springs, Colorado. Feeling the chill of the early morning, I cuddled into my coat as I waited for Dr. Barbara Shears, one of the region's highly respected doctors of naturopathic medicine, to return from shuttling her daughter to school. In her high-energy way, Barbara burst into the waiting room of her Victorian office/home with her youngest child riding her hip and ushered me to her spacious office. As I followed, I recalled the three years that this woman had tested and scanned me, needled and humored me (an essential combination), filled me with remedies and tinctures, guided me with wisdom and honesty.

We unbundled. Barbara set Travis on the floor to scoot, goo and coo his way among his toys and around the room – obviously a comfortable routine for the 10-month-old. "If you have to come before the nanny gets here, then the baby will be here," Barbara said as she settled behind her desk. "Most people don't care." And how could they when this vital 41-year-old makes herself so available to them – consulting, tending to healing crises and other emergencies between appointments and after hours. Not an easy job for a single mom of three. "I just do it," Barbara said candidly. "It's very simple. I have a big house, a part-time nanny, office help. I do it because it's right for me, it's fun – we're having fun."

Barbara's work also is challenging, and has been since its beginnings. When she graduated in 1979 from Oregon's National College of Naturopathic Medicine after completing its four-year program, there were no practicing women naturopaths in the United States. The holistic health field was immature at that time and, although the college taught natural healing, it was based on an allopathic (Western) model of health care. "There were no role models to say this is how you practice naturopathics or what it's about. I was on the forefront," she recalled. "That had its advantages in the sense that there were no limiting belief systems, and there were disadvantages in that there was no instruction on how to set up a practice, how to build a client base, how to practice all this eclectic mix of information you got. I kind of felt sorry for those first clients in Oregon because that's where I really learned what works and what doesn't work. It took me about four years to find a center point of naturopathic medicine and practice."

Barbara came by naturopathy naturally. "I felt like it fit more with my philosophical lifestyle beliefs at the time – whole foods, natural healing," she said. "It kind of grew out of that back-to-nature movement of the '60s. The main reason I became a naturopath was to do my own work. As I've done my own deeper healing – gone deeper into my own spiritual, mental, physical and emotional healing – that's what I teach, what my clients go through. You take them along with you."

Naturopathy uses nutrition, herbs, acupuncture and a variety of natural remedies and modalities to heal the body. Barbara begins by identifying and removing what she calls key physical-based interferences to one's wellness, such as foods and chemicals that cause a wide range of symptoms. "The body knows how to be healthy, it's the natural state," Barbara said. "The first step – the first program – involves eating right, exercising, lifestyle management changes. Then they start to feel that deeper resonance of health in their bodies and they like that." For some clients, she said, that's enough. But many others want to obtain and maintain an even deeper resonance in their lives and continue working with Barbara to identify other interferences or blocks, such as belief systems and behavior patterns.

How does Barbara identify interferences? With new clients, she uses muscle testing to verify her hunches because "it makes it more real to them when they can feel the actual weakness happen in their system," she explained. But most of the time she doesn't need to muscle test. "There's a feeling you get before you do the testing based on their symptoms, listening to them talk, being in their presence, scanning them psychically. I can't explain it, my experience is just knowing and I can reaffirm it with muscle testing. If the information is off, then you know that the person has a hidden agenda or is in deep denial. That can mean that they have a non-commitment to living and are saying 'I don't need help.' They have to have a commitment to life before you can even begin a program.

"Natural healing programs aren't easy – they are a major commitment," Barbara said. "They are a major commitment to your long-term health; they are a major commitment for people to be willing to experience pain, on whatever level that pain is. That's a hard one for a lot of people to stay present with. It's so easy in this culture to take drugs, to fix it. I'm sorry, there is no miracle cure – from drugs or supplements. A lot of people have been so sick before they came to me that they already made that shift, they already knew there wasn't going to be a quick fix or a miracle cure.

"When I talk to people I tell them it will take two years to get to step two. The first step is to get your physical body healthy enough to do anything else and it may take this much time, so they begin looking at the big picture. Then they have to start finding joy in the moment, joy in the dysfunction of the disease process itself. And of course when they find that place, the process goes faster. People I'm treating are starting out being quite ill. Others want fine tuning and deeper work. But since I'm as close to a medical doctor as one can get in the alternative health care field, I'm more of a first step – I'm pretty safe. I can start with a basic program and then begin sending them out to try other therapies from those further out in the alternative community."

Barbara refers people to acupuncturists, different types of bodyworkers – massage therapists, Rolfers, energy workers – and to a variety of non-traditional therapists who can help them work on their emotional, mental and spiritual needs. She also does acupuncture and energy work when called for, and prescribes homeo-pathic remedies and meditation exercises. "That's when we begin looking at how to bring consciousness or spiritual awareness all the way through the spirit body.

Then you can evolve because there's wellness, and then there's the evolution into a more conscious being. It's preventative medicine on all levels. We feel that this matches the evolution of our consciousness on this planet, and matches how Earth is evolving and changing – being in synch with all the other changes that the culture is going through."

One of Barbara's special interests is pre- and post-natal care, which stems from an earlier focus on obstetrics and her love of children. "I practiced obstetrics for four years but dropped it because I wanted to do private practice and have kids," Barbara said. She will, however, coordinate pre- and post-natal care with a midwife for those clients who prefer home births.

Throughout the interview, Barbara referred often to "we" – the collective body of healers that is starting to share and teach the concept of community. "It's like making your own tribe, to build a community of people whether it's your profession or belief system or friends," she explained. "Community is important in maintaining health on all levels. It's a concept we lost." Barbara's community offers balance to her type and style of work and enhances her personal growth as well. "I think most healers have gone through the same wounds. We're learning how to balance our wounds by being professionals, learning how to balance doing healing work and our own self-health care. If you don't do your own healing work then what are you mirroring to people? A lot of it is just being."

Although her pragmatic approach doesn't work

for everyone, this healer remains true to herself and notes that seeds are planted even if people don't return. "I'm not the kind of person to hold your hand through the whole thing – it's a different style. I really don't beat around the bush very much. I ask, how much are you committed to do this and do you want to do it?"

There's that word again – commitment. For Barbara it means the responsibility to each client's well-being. It's a commitment "to an intense method with people all day long," and it's her commitment to raising her family solo. "Having children is part of my path, part of my own healing." As for a partner, Barbara said, "He's in the future – eventually. It's all timing."

Rebecca Phillips
Doctor of Chiropractic

The philosophy of chiropractic is to open up blood or nerve flow. That's the fundamental view of Chinese medicine, as well. When life force or energy or chi flows evenly in sufficient quantity to all organs, then the body is well.

I sat on the edge of a treatment table in Dr. Rebecca Phillips' chiropractic clinic in Albuquerque, New Mexico, looking at my tongue in a hand mirror. Rebecca had looked at my tongue moments before and was drawing a picture as I observed my tongue's landscape. Same old rosy tongue with the cracks down the center. But something was different. "It's really swollen," I said, stunned by the oddity.

Rebecca referred to her drawing and said the swelling indicated "damp congestion" in my liver. The cracks corresponded to the spleen and pancreas and how they had been affected by poor bile production and/or distribution. She prescribed a Chinese herb for my liver and a supplement for my gall bladder. Then after she tested the flow of energy through my organ meridians, she handed me a food chart based on Chinese medicine that groups foods and flavors according to the organs they strengthen. "Focus first on the foods in the kidney column and the liver foods secondly," Rebecca said.

I drove north in the warm October sun pondering this wealth of information, reminded that we are what we eat, drink, breathe and think.

This brief sampling of Rebecca's work displayed how she gracefully dovetails chiropractic and Chinese medicine, something she has done in stages since she received her first acupuncture treatment in 1987. Her clinic is appropriately named Crossroads Chiropractic. "The philosophy of chiropractic is to open up blood or nerve flow. That's the fundamental view of Chinese medicine as well," said Rebecca, who graduated from Western States Chiropractic School in Oregon in 1984. "The underlying foundation of Chinese medicine and chiropractic is the concept of the life force that circulates within the body. When life force or energy or chi flows evenly in sufficient quantity to all organs, then the body is well. When there is excess or deficient energy flowing, there is dysfunction or ill health. Both models emphasize dynamics. To a chiropractor, health is full range of motion; to a Chinese physician, health is a balance of energy flow. Both review each symptom as part of the pattern that can only be understood within the context of the whole."

The Chinese diagnostic tools of observing the tongue and measuring energy flow through the meridians give Rebecca valuable information about a patient's symptoms or imbalances. Treatments might include electronic acupuncture and structural manipulation to open blocks in the energy flow and to reduce pain, addressing the emotions related to the weak organs, using Chinese herbs and Western supplements. "Nutrition and dietary changes are essential to the healing process, and this places responsibility on the patient," Rebecca said. "The Chinese say there are many solutions to restoring balance – you choose. Do you want to be treated from three to seven years, or do you want to be treated for three months?"

Rebecca developed an interest in Chinese medicine in the same way she discovered chiropractic:

She had a health problem and someone gave her a practitioner's name. She visited her first chiropractor while she was working as a researcher at Colorado State University's Comparative Oncology Unit in Fort Collins, Colorado. The chemicals she used daily in her cancer research had created skin and eye irritations, and the cortisone prescribed by medical doctors wasn't easing her symptoms – something that really didn't surprise her. (Her mother, a nurse, used only holistic medicine at home after Rebecca almost died at age 14 from mismanaged "walking pneumonia.") "A friend told me about this weird chiropractor who did muscle testing, magnet therapy and nutrition," Rebecca recalled. "I tried him and two days later my rash was gone. I was so impressed that six months later I was in chiropractor's school."

Chiropractor school, however, revealed that there were different kinds of chiropractic practices. "I went to school assuming that all chiropractors did weird things like this (Fort Collins) chiropractor did, and I found out that a lot of chiropractors were just bone crunchers and never really addressed the nutritional issues. The old chiropractors were holistic; the new ones were trying to fit themselves into the Western philosophy, and I didn't fit." A summer internship with an elderly chiropractor in Rebecca's home state of Kansas proved to be a turning point in her new career. "Dr. Cortner said he could make the lame walk and the blind see, and he did. He taught me acupuncture and nutrition; he taught me how to heal. Through him I realized that I wasn't crazy – that there were chiropractors out there like me."

Rebecca began her first practice in Hood River, Oregon, working solo because she didn't know any practitioners who shared her philosophy. Her patients had many allergies due to the damp climate. Her search for an anti-mucus medication and her personal need for physical balance (she had three miscarriages and was working non-stop) led her to Dr. Wai Tak Cheung in Portland, Oregon. "After seven treatments of acupuncture in three weeks and two weeks of drinking a tea, my son, Shane, was conceived and I never felt better in my life," Rebecca said. "I had a normal pregnancy and during the process I got rid of my back pain, my low blood pressure increased, my allergies were gone, I wasn't as nervous, and my hands and feet were warmer. All of those symptoms were related to my kidney being out of balance."

Dr. Cheung, who moved from China to Portland in 1949, is more than a doctor of Traditional Oriental Medicine. (Traditional Oriental Medicine incorporates practices from China, Japan and other Asian countries.) "He is a wise educator," Rebecca said. The "ageless" doctor encouraged her to come and study with him and to cut back her practice so she wouldn't put stress on her kidney. "During the process of working on me, he identified my interest or my abilities. He frequently takes on people from China and the U.S." With a full-time practice and a family to raise following the death of her first husband, Rebecca didn't have much time to spend with Dr. Cheung, so she would send patients to him along with her chiropractic diagnosis; he would share his diagnosis and treatment with her. Thus began their relationship of working long distance, which continues today.

"As time has gone on, I've learned a lot just by working with patients. I might not be there with Dr. Cheung, but I'm treating patients and he's telling me what to do over the phone. The Chinese way is that when you need an answer, you'll ask the right question. Until that question is asked, he doesn't give you the information. A lot of Chinese medicine is hands-on – you learn as you go. In old China, the doctors talked to one another; the older ones showed the younger ones how to do things. Dr. Cheung's office was much like that, too, with younger doctors following him around."

Rebecca received certification in electronic acupuncture from the International Academy of Clinical Acupuncture in 1987. She described the Chinese-issued certification as a chiropractic approach to acupuncture and a fast way to get training. Her method of acupuncture involves holding an electric stimulus on the acupuncture point that does not break the skin. "It gives immediate pain release and short-term energy balance, so I don't feel a need to use needles," she said. If patients need more intensive work, they are referred to an acupuncturist.

She also spent two weeks in China with a group of chiropractors observing Chinese medical practices in a hospital setting. Although she had been learning about Chinese herbs, she didn't begin using them in her practice until she moved to Albuquerque two years ago. The licensing laws in New Mexico gave her the freedom to combine her eclectic training in Oriental medicine with chiropractic – something she was unable to do in Oregon.

The Chinese approach to treatment is very simple and uses fundamental criteria based on nature and energy, Rebecca said. "The Chinese don't separate body, mind and spirit. Everything is in harmony according to Mother Nature." The Chinese way also involves the patient. After Rebecca does tongue diagnosis, which she shows the patient how to do, she uses an electronic device called a Rodarocu, an instrument developed by the Koreans or Japanese (depending on whom you talk to, she said) to measure the energy flow at an acupuncture point. "It's diagnostic and therapeutic. In other words, you read out the energy and then you treat the imbalance. Then you read it out again and continue to treat. It enables you to show the patient visually what acupuncture is doing."

The Rodarocu also enables patients to see what organs are out of balance so they can gain a deeper understanding of their healing process. There are five major organ systems – liver, heart, spleen, lung and kidney – and each is associated with an emotion, a sense, a season and foods of a particular flavor, temperature and color. For example, kidney is associated with fear, winter and hearing. Foods that nurture the kidney are salty, warming and dark in color, such as kidney beans, cranberries, wheat, walnuts and shellfish.

Too much stress to the kidneys can cause anxiety, tiredness and other symptoms; further imbalance comes from ingesting too many cold foods and drinks, and using too many or not enough dark, salty foods.

So diet becomes a big part of a patient's healing. In China it represents 50 percent of the process, Rebecca said. "In Chinese medicine, food is the first line of defense. They resort to medication only when food fails to effect a cure. There are foods for cure when you are really out of balance; there are foods for maintenance. Simple things like drinking warm water when your kidney's cold can greatly enhance the kidney's ability to heal. If a patient is not willing to change their diet, they can be given herbs to overcome what they're creating through their diet. But it takes much longer to correct the problem. Americans are very impatient, so I often use digestive enzymes to assist in the process."

Patients also are encouraged to receive other therapies that enhance energy flow, such as massage or cranial-sacral work. (She knows firsthand the healing effects of massage, since she was certified in massage therapy before she went to chiropractic school.) And for patients who want to become more involved in their healing process, Rebecca offers weekend seminars where she combines lecture with hands-on healing.

Rebecca seems as eager to educate others as she is to expand her own knowledge of healing practices. Teaching a variety of seminars throughout the country gives her private practice balance, she said. Her personal life also appears to be in balance, and she receives support from her husband, Andy, who helped run her office when she first opened. It all comes down to energy for this vital 43-year-old, who moves briskly and with intention through her world. "I was born a kidney personality – tend to go, go, go. I was probably exhausted by the time I went to Chinese medicine. My hair was starting to gray at 35 and acupuncture reversed all of that. Now I nurture my kidney, take kidney tonics. The secrets of being able to do what we do as physicians include learning how to nurture our kidneys. Sometimes rest is the only thing that replenishes the kidneys."

As I observed Rebecca the morning of our visit, it was obvious that her philosophy and lifestyle support her. The drive into town from her mountain home east of Albuquerque helps prepare her for a demanding practice. Some days, she has a steady stream of patients and little time for herself. But when her workday ends and she drives home with her son in tow, she feels a sense of freedom she didn't have with her previous practice. Chinese medicine has taught her how to keep her professional and personal lives in harmony.

Healer update

Dr. Rebecca Phillips now uses earth essences to clear energy blocks from the emotional body so the physical body can be healed. Rebecca makes her own earth or stone essences and uses the remedies in the form of sprays and creams.

Contact information

Dr. Rebecca Phillips
Crossroads Chiropractic
2632 Pennsylvania NE
Suite D
Albuquerque, NM 87100
office: (505) 291-9800
fax: (505) 291-1234

Xiaorong "Linda" Li
Doctor of Oriental Medicine

The human body is like a house. When we want to know what's going on with the internal organs, we use the five senses to give us information. Those are our windows.

Nearly 300 large glass jars, each filled with a different wild herb from China, line the walls of Dr. Xiaorong Li's reception room in Albuquerque, New Mexico. Roots, barks, stems, caps and flowers present themselves in a myriad of forms and colors. Some are delicately patterned in soft earth tones; others are deeper tones of earth and sea. Brightly colored boxes of patented herbs, prepared and packaged in China, complete the pharmacopoeia that is available to patients as well as walk-in customers.

Xiaorong, who adopted Linda as her American name, uses herbs along with acupuncture and other traditional Chinese treatments at the Chinese Natural Healing Clinic. The energetic 32-year-old also teaches at the International Institute of Chinese Medicine in Santa Fe, which she said provides a healthy balance to her practice. "Most acupuncturists in this town are very, very busy and don't have time to do research. Teaching is good because I can practice English, update Traditional Chinese Medicine information and study further."

Many Chinese doctors – particularly the older ones, Linda said – who visit or practice medicine in America, speak little or no English. Linda expresses herself clearly in English, but her beginnings in this country did not come with ease. Linda's husband was working on his doctorate at New Mexico State University in Las Cruces when she joined him in 1987. "When I came here from China, my English was not as good as it is now, and I was not able to practice Chinese medicine. After two or three years, my English was much better and I found the teaching job in Santa Fe. That really helped my English, and after working there for two semesters, I was able to start my own practice."

Linda's purpose in America also unfolded as her career evolved. "I'm bridging a gap, connecting the two cultures," she said, carefully choosing her words. We spoke on a fall afternoon at her office, while her son and husband played in the background. The directness with which she spoke was softened by her graceful and reflective manner. "Before I came to this country, I didn't know many people interested in Traditional Chinese Medicine and thought I would have to change my career and perhaps practice only Western medicine. Since I stayed here, I'm finding that teaching has made the difference. Most important to me is teaching and introducing Chinese medicine in this country. In China there are a lot of people, and I'm not so important. In America, they need a lot of people like me."

Linda's desire to be a doctor was seeded by her parents, who were medical doctors in China. They practiced Western medicine rather than Traditional Chinese Medicine (TCM), but her mother walked a middle road, Linda said, and used foods to enhance the healing process. When Linda decided to become a doctor, her father offered his 35-year-old medical library but she declined to take it. "I chose Traditional Chinese Medicine because it is more natural. I wanted to make people feel good without side effects. And Chinese medicine can heal diseases that Western medicine can't."

The TCM college Linda attended after

undergraduate school focused on Western medicine for the first two years, then devoted the next three years to Chinese medicine. Her degree enables her to practice both Western and Chinese medicines in China, which she did while working at a traditional Chinese medical research hospital. She later practiced only TCM.

One of the things that Linda wants to emphasize through practicing and teaching TCM is that acupuncture is more than inserting needles. "If a person comes to you with a headache, you have to find the reason for the headache. Just because the head aches doesn't mean you needle the head. If you want to practice TCM, you have to know more than just the acupuncture points. You have to know the whole TCM theory, to collect a lot of detailed information that will lead you to the symptom's cause.

"When Chinese medicine developed in ancient China, doctors didn't have ultrasound or labs to do tests. They observed Mother Nature's changes, all the natural phenomena, and applied it to the human body. In Chinese medicine the body is like nature, it's organic. When the sun rises, you wake up and become active; then the sun goes down and you fall asleep. The whole theory of yin and yang was created throughout many, many generations of studying relationships in nature.

"There is a philosophy that says if you want to know what's inside a house you look in the door and windows and what you see and smell gives you information. The human body is like a house. When we want to know what's going on with the internal organs, we use the five senses to give us information. Those are our windows."

Using the five senses means that the practitioner uses her mouth for communication; her eyes to observe the way the patient acts and looks, taking special note of breathing, tongue color and texture, eyes and skin; touch to feel the organ pulses located in both wrists; the ears to listen to the patient's voice and breath; the nose to detect any body odors. Pulse and tongue diagnosis are central to Traditional Chinese Medicine.

Linda used the common ailment of back pain as an example. "In collecting the medical history, you ask if the pain is chronic or acute – has it been there for five years or two weeks? Age is important, the origin of the pain, its quality – dull, sharp. Does it move around – movement is associated with wind; is it aggravated by hot or cold? You consider their constitution and that the kidneys are in the lower back. Then I make the diagnosis. It might be due to qi (energy) and blood stagnation or to kidney deficiency. But most people who come to me have more than that. There are other problems that haven't bothered these people yet. We may need to work on the liver and spleen, too. We don't just treat disease but we prevent it. That's why Chinese medicine treats the human body as an organic whole. We treat the root, the organs that cause the symptoms. When the organ is stronger, the whole body is harmonized and balanced and people become well."

Treatments generally take two to eight weeks (chronic conditions may take longer) and combine acupuncture with patented herbs or wild herbs that patients prepare at home as teas (many taste horrible, Linda said). She also does food therapy and recommends exercise and stress reduction programs. Other therapies like cupping and moxibustion might be used. (Cupping is the use of glass suction cups that are placed on the skin to remove excess moisture from the body. Moxibustion directs heat into the body by placing a burning cigar-like stick of rolled paper and herbs over vital acupuncture points.)

Internal medicine and gynecology are Linda's specialties. She works a lot with menstrual problems like endometriosis and with infertility, which she said are caused by qi and blood stagnation in the uterus or qi deficiency in the kidneys or spleen. She proudly points to two cases where women have become pregnant through treatments at her clinic. And one man, whom she treated for back pain for two months, not only boasted that his pain and tiredness went away but that he had increased hair growth.

"Kidney is associated with hair growth," Linda said. "So if kidney energy is strong, hair growth will be strong. Long-term clinic practice and information passed on through generations shows that the kidney and ear have a very close relationship and that the liver and eye are related. TCM is a science, not superstition; it's not esoteric. It follows the classic, traditional medicine book that was discovered 2,000 years ago. Some of the records date back 5,000 years. It's like our bible. If there are questions, we go back and follow what it said. We don't develop our own idea in Chinese medicine."

So when Linda gives acupuncture treatments she goes by the book and selects the needle points based on the diagnosis. She leaves needles in for 30 to 40 minutes for more stubborn conditions; 20 to 25 minutes for milder conditions. But how does she know that the needles are working? "If the patient feels a heavy, dull, achy or numb feeling in the area, that's good and the needle is working. Sometimes they feel sensations moving along the meridians, which is good because qi flows. The patient can feel energy or 'arriving qi' moving. The doctor also can feel energy moving through the handle of the needle. It's like fishing. You put the hook in the water and you can feel that it's heavier. Same thing: You put in the needle, manipulate it, and it feels heavier. It's like going into a vacuum – you can't take the needle out until the energy is balanced."

It's important for Linda to balance her own energy as well, which she does by following Chinese medicine. Even though she said she's always been healthy, she's conscientious about doing things that work for her. She cooks Chinese food and uses organic produce when possible, does self-acupressure for tune-ups and maintenance, practices Tai Chi for exercise and Qi Gong, a form of meditation that incorporates mind and breathing exercises. Since she works six days a week and has a family (the Lis' 5-year-old son is quite at home at the clinic), Linda said she is careful not to get overstressed, gets massage occasionally and is cautious about letting acupuncture students work on her.

As time permits, Linda wants to expand her role in bringing Chinese medicine to America. "I want to introduce more Chinese information to this country – a lot of information hasn't been translated into English. And I want to write books on women's health – PMS, menopause, infertility, irregular menstruation, and dysmenorrhea – not just for TCM students but for the public. I'd like my private practice to grow, but still keep a balance with my family. And in the future, I would like to have a school. I really enjoy teaching, and students seem very satisfied with my explanations. They want to know more information than what's written in a book."

Linda helped edit "Herbalist Handbook," a recently published book on Chinese herbs, and has on occasion been an interpreter for guest teachers from China. Despite the language barriers and sometimes foreign concepts, Linda strongly believes TCM can serve anyone. "It works for all human beings. Constitutions may be different, but the diagnosis principles are the same. Nature's elements are everywhere. We're all human beings."

Healer update

Dr. Linda Li's practice now also serves patients insured by various health care providers.

Linda continues to receive invitations to speak to groups of Western medical doctors and to the general public because of her ability to explain Traditional Chinese Medicine. She still teaches at the International Institute of Chinese Medicine.

Contact Information

Dr. Linda Li
Chinese Natural Healing Clinic
1517 Eubank NE
Albuquerque, NM 87112
(505) 294-7368

PART TWO

NUTRITIONISTS AND HERBAL
PRACTITIONERS

Judith Lilly
Holistic Nutritionist

What I'm here to do is to help people discover who we really are – individually and collectively – and my work is the tool I use to do it.

Judith Lilly considers herself Colorado Springs' most gentle nutritionist. "I'm about as gentle as they come in town. I'm soft, yielding," Judith said, then added with a laugh, "and totally in left field – out there." Her gentleness can be seen in her loving blue-green eyes, heard in her caring, soft-spoken words, felt in her touch when she lightly "dances" with her client's energy field, gathering data and confirming her observations.

Home and work environments, however, have not always been gentle with this midwife-turned-nutritionist. Nor has she always been gentle with herself. For example, when 26 and pregnant, Judith decided to "abort her husband" (after he changed his mind about having a child) and join the U.S. Army. "I just needed a major shift in my life and jumped off the edge of the cliff to do it," she said. And in the nearly 10 years that she was involved in midwifery, Judith was "busted" twice for practicing without a license.

Today, Judith works out of her turn-of-the-century home/office where clients are greeted by her equally gentle (but not so petite) canine companion, Montana, and sometimes by her teen-age daughter. Her life at 42 seems calm and well-balanced compared to her years as an Army hospital surgical technician and midwife-crusader. But it was those experiences that propelled this 5-foot dynamo along the path of healer with a special interest in women.

Appalled by the lack of information available to women when she worked at an Army hospital's labor and delivery ward for more than a year, Judith set out to educate women about ways to care for themselves and protect themselves from unnecessary medical procedures. She began teaching home birth classes and joined a network of midwives-in-training and doctors who were performing home births.

Judith reluctantly joined a friend – a midwife apprentice – in caring for 40 expecting couples after three home birth doctors were charged with malpractice. The two women continued to practice midwifery for several years. But since midwifery wasn't legalized in Colorado Springs, Colorado, until 1993, the team eventually faced its own legal charges (which later were dropped) and Judith faced her own personal crisis.

"The second time I got busted – that was in the mid-1980s – I got very sick," Judith recalled. "It had to do with self-esteem, issues with authority, having my livelihood taken away." Her ill health led her to Colorado Springs nutritionist Vivian Rice, who helped her heal and look at the mental patterns that were manifesting in illness. Part of her recovery involved writing an affirmation or "letter of manifestation" that enabled her to redirect her work and develop a new support system on all levels. It's a powerful tool she encourages clients to use.

"I asked to work in a holistic profession, with people of like mind who are willing to do their homework and make movement in their life; to be supported by my community, to be middle class, to be able to expand my learning at all points, to continue with my own work. And I hadn't a clue what it would look like." Not long afterwards, Vivian invited Judith to be her apprentice. During the year and a half that followed, Judith learned muscle testing (something she encourages her clients to do), nutrition theory, the mental/emotional causes of ill health, herbology, and "glimmers" of homeopathy, energy medicines and bodywork. She worked as Vivian's partner for four years before starting her own practice in holistic nutrition and expanding her healing tools to include more homeopathy, various forms of energy work (Jin Shin and Polarity, to mention a few) and massage therapy.

What Judith terms as the "out-there" aspect of her practice is simply the application of her personal belief system and her gifts of grace, which began taking form while she was a midwife. "You come to a point in life where you have the physical stuff down – or at least you think you do – and you start delving into the mental and emotional. And when you've got that in your pocket, then you can move into the spiritual stuff. It's a natural evolution. So that's when I started talking to babies in utero and to their spirits with their moms. The mother and I hold hands and as I meditate the baby talks to me through words, visions or its movements."

She practiced reading the auras of Vivian's four-legged clients (dogs and cats) as she built trust in her new vision. Meditation helped her separate a voice of guidance from "the committee" (mental chatter), while a psychic helped her to understand how she could access information from past lives. Continued use of affirmations enabled her to obtain higher levels of clarity.

Judith uses this clarity – in the form of "guided readings" – when she communicates with a client's higher self during her 30- and 60-minute sessions. "I get most of my information from wakeful guided information and through muscle testing. I'll muscle test to see if I'm on the right track or if there's something else I need to do with the information I've intuited. It's all timing – how much to tell clients, what to do with the information." Judith is cautious not to overwhelm new clients with this type of information or to usurp their power. "What I want to do is to empower them in their healing. So I talk to them about listening to their inner selves, which will sound like inner truths rather than a brand new class in metaphysics."

"When people come to see me, I ask them what they need and start from there. I run through all of their glands and systems, all of their physical complaints, where they are physically from split ends and cuticles to having a hysterectomy. What I tell them in theory is that death is the end of disease – dis-ease, surgery is one step back from that, having to take drugs is one back from that, herbs is one back from that, food is one back from that, the other is total optimal health. Pretty holistic.

"What I try to do is bring them backwards through that chain of health and get them back to where diet, good thinking, right lifestyle and a few herbs will get them through. That's my goal. I always tell them that not everyone can reach that goal, that they may have too much damage or not be able to extricate themselves from their lifestyle for one reason or another. Or perhaps it's not their choice in life."

Most of Judith's clients are women "because that's what I'm good at. I feel like I understand women and women's issues, and they are my teachers as well. They are invested in their healing and the healing of the planet." Many clients come to her in crisis as a last resort because the medical profession has not been able to help them. Some come with "nagging" problems, while others "just come in because they're supposed to be here, they need fluffing," she said eyeing this writer.

(I immediately recall the powerful – and surprising – effects of a homeopathic remedy she prescribed for me several months ago. Fluff, I laugh. Fine-tuning may be a better word, which gives more latitude to the kinds of symptoms experienced while the body normalizes and heals. And she and I both know that my body – anybody's body – wouldn't ask for something it couldn't handle. Natural healing, after all, often means that symptoms may get worse before they get better, especially with homeopathic remedies. What Judith calls fluff is the support and nurturing she offers to those who have a deeper commitment to health, "who need an affirmation of themselves and what they're doing.")

Judith laughs in her impish way and continues: "I feel like a lot of what I'm here to do is to help people discover who we really are – individually and collectively – and my work is the tool I use to do it. My goal is to bring anyone who is ready up to where I am and guide them past me. If that goal can't be reached, I assist them as far as they can go in a safe way. For those more evolved on their path, I feel like my purpose is to assist in their refinement and to support them in that. People on that level who are working with oneness and moving into grace usually are pulling together all of their past lives as well, to bring all of their information into fruition in this lifetime so they can have completion and enlightenment. That means the physical forms get hit kind of hard, so I talk to them about supporting the physical – balancing the physical and spiritual."

When appropriate, Judith shares her belief system based on a set of laws – survival, Mother Nature, religion, karma and grace – which she has compiled from many teachers along her journey. In order to live in balance, she believes that all laws must be embraced and moved through in order to achieve a state of oneness.

Although Judith seems solid in her state of grace, she has had her share of "physical stuff" – eczema and a "deep-seated, fear-based virus" like chronic fatigue syndrome – and still works hard at maintaining balance. Her illnesses and unhealthy choices in relationships have been her teachers, for which she is grateful. She shares home with her companion of five years and works at home so she can be available to her daughter. Equally important, she wants clients to meet her furry friend, Montana, "because he's part of who I am." (Her clientele still includes dogs and cats.) Judith regularly connects with other healers in her community, works a job outside her profession one day a week for variety and plays in the great outdoors whenever possible. She has a line of herbal tinctures and makes some of them from her own homegrown herbs.

This gentle and spritely Capricorn, who thought her life's work was midwifery, now wonders what may follow her current career choice. "I do have the great will to change something – I believe I can change anything. But I'm still working on believing that I can."

Healer update

Judith Lilly has added essential oils to her many offerings.

She plans to teach apprenticeship classes and is considering interested individuals for an apprenticeship in her practice.

Contact information

Judith Lilly
Judith Lilly Nutrition
2022 Armstrong Ave.
Colorado Springs, CO 80904
(719) 471-3822
email: judylilly@att.net

Judith Yarrow
Health Consultant/Nutritionist

I've had a lot of groups from around the country come and seek visions out here. I feel it's like a window that helps people open to that different place inside themselves.

As I wait for Judith Yarrow to finish a telephone consultation, I scan the vast openness that surrounds her rural home. It's early January and the high plains are dry and brown. Winter comes early and stays late in these parts, and snow blankets this little valley north of Palmer Lake, Colorado.

"The reason why I'm here is to bring people back to nature," Judith said as we settled into her sun-filled office. She and her companion, Larry Lawn, have been developing and expanding the property's offerings since they moved here from Colorado Springs three years ago. "I was guided to this piece of land – I really sense that the angels brought me here. Living in the city was beginning to compromise my vitality, and I felt that I needed a much closer connection to the earth. Pretty much everything that's here is what I put out to the universe. A lot of my work is about working co-creatively with Spirit."

Judith's offerings are many. For the past 15 years, she has worked in bio-energetic nutrition, hydrotherapy, herbology, Reiki and flower essence and aromatherapy repatterning. And like many others in the healing field, Judith unconsciously began her career as a healer in her late 20s when she used nutrition to heal her pre-arthritic symptoms and depression. Then she studied with a herbalist who had just healed his cancer, "and it just fired up my soul," Judith recalled. "I was out in the field studying plants all of the time, started teaching herb classes. I just studied and studied – you name it, I took it."

When Judith became a single mom after a short-lived marriage, she began working in clinics and continuing her on-the-job studies and personal awakening. She became certified in various clinical techniques, such as live cell analysis (a form of blood analysis) and colon therapy, before she started the string of businesses that led to her current practice.

But what led me, like many others, to Judith is the spiritual work she does individually and with groups through flower essences and the Transformation Game, a box game created by the Findhorn community in Scotland. "Findhorn and flower essences are two things I was connected to many years ago. I've always felt a core connection with communities like Findhorn and flower essences, and find them to be planned so nicely because they both really work with attuning the spirit. Even though I use very physical types of programs in my practice, my love is working with flower essences. When I read Dr. (Edward) Bach's information 10 or 12 years ago, I felt quite an affinity to his sensitivity to and awareness of the mental, emotional and spiritual ramifications of illness. It's very much an important part of my program with people.

"My work is very much associated with healing the soul," Judith continued. "Of course a lot of people come in the door with nutrition or something specific to approach. And I can do lab work and the clinical tests they need to see for validation. Those pieces of information are important to people, help to ground them. The more evolved energies I'm working towards need that kind of anchor, so it's a real good blending. I feel that I'm a real master of blending those pieces in a way that really works. It's later on when people are open to their own essence that I can say, 'You know, we really are doing a great deal more here than nutrition. We're talking about bringing through who you really are, and about your soul's purpose, its intention.' I tend to work with very doubtful persons. A lot of times people just need to be heard."

Judith uses muscle testing and intuition to determine which flower essences and other therapies her clients need and selects the essences from more than a dozen trays of small bottles. There are the 38 Bach Flower Remedies, numerous American flower essences; essences derived from minerals, and her newest and "extremely powerful" Starlight Elixirs. The liquid in each bottle holds the spiritual essence of its source, which is carefully extracted by infusing the flower or mineral in liquid. The Starlight Elixirs are formulated by transferring the energy pattern of a star through a sophisticated telescope into a container of liquid suspended in front of the eyepiece.

Each essence works in cooperation with a person's emotional, mental or spiritual needs, and facilitates healing by increasing awareness, releasing blocks and restoring balance, Judith explained. "I find the flower essences to be a wonderful tool. People experience a lot of personal growth when working with essences. The Bach flower essences tend to work with people's deep inherited core patterns from previous generations – a lot of fears, angers, things we brought with us. The American flower essences address a much more expanded level, which includes creativity and freedom. Other companies address many other issues, other levels. It's exciting to watch the effects of the flower essences on people who are really stuck, therapy-resistant and have unhealthy lifestyles. It enables me to plant seeds with their unconscious about anything underlying their condition, then over the months that follow see a profound softening. A door opens, they hear you. That's really profound work."

Judith also markets her own blends of flower essences – a massage formula used both orally and topically to help break up energy blocks, and a cleansing and protection spray for therapists. And she's beginning to use flower essences with people who play the Transformation Game and other groups with which she does healing and visionary work. By muscle testing the group, she said, "you get a combination of essences that really brings out what that group's energy is about. It can be very powerful."

She has led various rites-of-passage ceremonies for teen-agers, and works with a wide range of professional groups. One of her most moving experiences was with a group of Soviet physicians and physicists, and a group of Catholic nuns who came from throughout the country to gather in her tepee. Judith said an angel spoke to her during each group's meditation and offered valuable information pertaining to their goals and intentions. She doesn't consider herself a psychic but feels divinely guided. "The information is just there, comes from a place of knowing," she said. "I like to see people empower themselves and am helping them to open up that information in themselves. Yet the knowingness and magic is very much a part of my life."

That "knowingness" or intuition guided Judith when she interpreted the function of each of the flower essences used in my elixir. It is present when she facilitates the Transformation Game, helping players understand the information that is being mirrored to them. "The game is really phenomenal, is divinely inspired. It provides a really safe container for people to work at their physical, mental, emotional and spiritual elements and to take responsibility for these elements in a loving, playful and cooperative way that most family systems don't do. Findhorn is very much out in the forefront of what we're going to see established all over the planet because of the example they demonstrate: community and working co-creatively with nature."

Judith wants to focus more on teaching community skills, she said, "because a lot of what I do is about community." She and Larry, who also is a game facilitator, plan to bring in Findhorn trainers to direct a large group in playing the planetary game. "The planetary game helps you see how you play your life out in relationship to the planet and other people, how your actions affect the planet."

The planet. Judith cannot escape her growing relationship and responsibility to it. "This piece of land (where she lives) is on a major vortex of energy, a matrix point. There are a lot of matrix points being established on the Earth as a new energy pattern gets established. The energy is coming from the Earth and the universe, both ways, and it takes human intervention to develop it. These are new energy centers – not old blocked areas – which we're establishing. In my meditations, I was asked to bring people here. That's why I put the teepee in. I've had a lot of groups from around the country come and seek visions out here. I feel it's like a window that helps people to open to that different place inside themselves."

Plans for the land, which Judith and Larry don't own, include restoring natural fishing ponds and an unusual concrete and rock pool that reminds Judith of a baptismal pool, rebuilding the barn and adding structures that recognize different religious and spiritual beliefs. Already in frequent use are the medicine wheel and sweat lodges, which appear to be guarded by two metal sculptures. "I'm excited and scared about putting the next pieces together. I'm just trusting. I want to make our place available to different expressions, including music, movement, art, and to bring in goddess energy."

Judith acknowledges the tiring pace she has been keeping the past few years (she admits it's part of her Aries nature), but welcomes the next phase. On this land or somewhere else, she knows the angels will continue to guide her. After all, she offered with a laugh, "I don't have anything else to do."

Healer update

Judith Yarrow added aromatherapy and the clown, "Amazing Grace," to her practice.

Clinical studies that prove the healing effects of essential oils and laughter have opened doors for their use in more traditional settings. Judith currently uses her aromatherapy program at a hospital hospice. Her healing work includes "sacred clown" skits, storytelling and music.

Her private practice is now mobile – she and her husband live in one recreational vehicle; she conducts her practice in another. They plan to travel to "traumatized" areas of the country and offer healing services.

Contact Information

Judith Yarrow
Health Enhancement
P.O. Box 6910
Colorado Springs, CO 80934
voice mail: (719) 386-7140
email: yarrowj@aol.com
website: www.youngliving.net/herbalrenewal

Cathy Hope
Apothecary

I see myself as an agent of change – someone who is trying to tune into natural rhythms and helping others to tune into natural rhythms.

Apothecary Cathy Hope planted her first garden when she was 8 years old. Cathy "bugged and bugged and bugged" her mother until she was granted her very own spot, which she later learned was the least desirable plot in the backyard. Then for a couple of years, Cathy "stole" flowers from her mother's garden and planted them in her own.

"I didn't know what I was doing. But I'd talk to the plants and tell them what I was doing, where they were going and how beautiful they were," Cathy recalled, as we spent a wintry afternoon seated by the wood-burning stove in her country home north of Taos, New Mexico. "One of the things that I remember noticing as a child was how nature worked – you know, with the leaves and stuff. I just piled leaves on the garden every winter, and whenever I would transplant I would crumble up leaves and stick them at the bottom of the hole and then plant the flowers."

Cathy's eyes sparkled, her grin widened as she embraced the memory. "I had this intuitive understanding of what they would like. Then I would praise them, just love them. My mother never got angry with me because she was just so amazed at how well my garden would do. I remember feeling great joy." Cathy also observed how plants responded to the Pennsylvania seasons, how their growth varied from year to year, and the sequence in which flowers bloomed. "It was like a biological clock. I had a sense of participating in the rhythm of nature just by observing. In a sense, that's my entire ground of being, why I do what I do. I don't remember if plants talked back, I just remember that I felt good doing it."

At 42, Cathy still embodies that joy of her youth. Her high-desert garden – rich with decomposing leaves and a thriving earthworm population – produces more than flowers, however. Last summer she grew and harvested herbs to combine with other natural and organic ingredients in her homemade tinctures and liniments. The herbal tinctures are a recent addition to the diverse offerings of Cathy's 12-year-old company, Iris Herbal Products. Her natural herbal preparations – all guided by "a synthesis of science and intuition" – also include blends of essential oils and flower essences, potpourris, salves, lotions and magic-making potions.

"I consider myself an apothecary, a maker of herbal medicines. I don't diagnose, I don't treat. I listen and make suggestions based on common sense, and I refer people to professionals," Cathy said. And when the self-taught herbalist isn't sharing her knowledge with clients, customers or students – "It's such a pleasure to talk about what gives me so much joy and what I've dedicated my life to" – she is reading, researching, experimenting and inventing.

Cathy began her relationship with herbs when she "fell into" a job developing the herb department of a food co-operative in Atlanta, Georgia. She was in her 20's at the time, coming from the Appalachian Mountains of Virginia where she had been a potter for six years. "It feels like I never in my whole life sat down and asked myself what I was going to do. I always felt led or dropped into situations," she said. In keeping with that pattern, working with herbs led her to the co-op's produce department – a job that transformed her and the produce section. "Very little was being grown organically and sold to stores at the time. Our warehouse had been carrying organic produce from Florida for some time, which gave me the idea to expand by bringing in produce from California. It was all new, and I was very vital, energetic and idealistic."

Then Cathy had a dream – one of two spiritual events that changed the course of her life. "The upshot of the dream was that you are your own spirit guide, you are your own path. You can't get that from anyone else," she said. About a year later, in 1979, the second happening occurred while Cathy was receiving one of her weekly massages. "A voice speaks in my right ear and says `That would be so much more effective if she were using essential oils,'" Cathy recalled in animated fashion. "'What are essential oils?' I thought, this is too weird. No one is going to believe me. Also being a Taurus, I wasn't sure if I even believed in energy."

Cathy's second experience prompted her to take a break from her job and spend five months living in a teepee in the backwoods of Tennessee, "getting in touch with things I felt as a child." When she returned to her job, she also returned to the chiropractic care and massage therapy that enabled her petite body to keep up with the job's physical demands. During that time she also read books on aromatherapy and the energetics of plants. Robert B. Tissarand's first book, "The Art of Aromatherapy," had just been published. "I was so impressed, I bought some essential oils and just kept reading every single book, pamphlet or article I could find."

And she began experimenting. She decided to start with salves and tried each of the five recipes she had collected. "They varied from runny to hard. I just took the middle path between the two extremes and got a salve body that I really liked. Then I looked at Tiger Balm, the only thing on the market like it back then, and said I could do that, too." (She calls her version Starfire's Balm.) "It felt good doing it, felt good using it, and I liked smelling it. I thought, this is so exciting."

After she perfected salves, Cathy began experimenting with blending essential oils and carrier oils (base oils such as sweet almond and apricot kernel) for massage therapists. She took the blends, the "works in progress," with her on her first visit west to New Mexico in 1982 and gathered feedback from people she met through friends. "It really evolved from there," she said.

Two years later a friend who had a massage practice in Florida asked Cathy to make some chakra oils. Cathy didn't know what chakras were, and all her friend would say was that she was working with chakras and needed oils for them. Once again, Cathy plunged herself into study, reading about different cultures and the different energies they attached to flowers. "This is all energetics, not what they do physically, physiologically or pharmaceutically. It's about what their energy is, what organs they gravitate to and heal."

It took months to compile information about the traditions of energy systems used by the cultures she targeted in Africa, India, China and Europe. Cathy was obsessed by it. When she finally found enough similarities in cultural practices, she created 24 oils and circulated them through her network of massage therapists. In the two years that followed, she developed two sets or kits of chakra oils. One kit "helps to open chakras, move energy upward and increase awareness," while the other "helps harmonize and balance chakras." "They are very powerful and effective," Cathy said. "And they smell wonderful." (I know, I use some of them.)

Iris Herbal Products became a full-time business in 1988 after Cathy moved to the Taos area. She came out for a conference, fell in love with the land, then fell in love with her companion of five years. "It's so trite," Cathy laughed. (That's when I met Cathy. She was promoting her products at a fair in Taos. I tried her massage oil blends for a while and returned to them recently when I discovered that the quality of her product was superior to others I had used. And I liked the personal notes she attached to order forms.)

Since the birth of her company, Cathy has learned the joy of expressing herself through her work. She strives to balance Iris Herbal's expansion with integrity, to keep harmony in her life and on the planet. "As an apothecary working with herbal medicines, my intention is to do no harm – no harm to the person or to the particular plant, species or environment."

Cathy orders essential oils from more than a dozen different companies. Her criteria: plants that have been grown organically or wildcrafted from natural habitats and that have been processed carefully and respectfully. "It's an art – a science that's really an art. It matters the time of day and year a plant is picked; it matters what species is used, because they all smell different and have different healing properties. What goes on your skin is as important as what goes in your mouth." And she wants people to smell only the best fragrances: The orange-scented neroli that carries one to the family farm in Italy where it was picked; "the lemon that smells like a room full of fresh lemons, or the ginger that smells like it is right in front of you." Cathy could go on and on, breathing in fragrant memories as she talks.

Many wild plants like goldenseal are in danger, Cathy said, so she is careful to purchase herbs from wildcrafters and organic growers who are not over-harvesting. She also is developing herbal combinations that are more symptom-specific and is spending time educating clients and customers on the benefits of synergistic combinations.

Her own healing process has taught Cathy the importance of gentleness. When she speaks of "no harm to the person," she refers to herbs that tone or strengthen one's system – herbs she emphasizes in her catalog. Herbs that detoxify are equally important, but should be taken with caution. Using detoxifying methods with herbs and fasts at the beginning of one's healing program can sometimes create problems, she said, especially if not used under the care of an herbalist or naturopath.

"People are looking for a magic bullet and there isn't one. So I started searching for a way I could give them something that would help without exacerbating existing conditions. There are all kinds of therapeutic formulas that other companies are making that are excellent. I didn't want to compete or duplicate, so I focused on areas I was personally familiar with, like tonification. I looked for herbs and herbal combinations that increase vitality, viability or mechanical function and support of that organ system."

Cathy's focus on respiratory ailments, the immune system, the liver and menopause has directed her to study herbs like American and Chinese ginseng (the properties of these plants are somewhat different, she said), and the synergistics of echinacea and other herbs. "I see myself as an agent of change – someone who is trying to tune into natural rhythms and helping other people tune into natural rhythms. People get sick, want to get well. That's a natural rhythm."

Her knowledge of plants and their medicinal properties seems endless. Several hours by the wood stove slipped by before we ventured across Cathy's front yard to the garage-like structure where she makes her magic. A dreamy blend of fragrance wafted from the door as we entered. Cathy fluttered about her workshop like a fairy as she poured essential oils into amber-colored bottles and offered me a whiff of this and a sniff of that. Her eyes grew big. She giggled. Once again, Cathy had entered the world she knew as a child, a place of joy and harmony. Now, through Iris Herbal, she has found a way to share it with others.

Healer update

Cathy Hope has expanded her tincture line to more than 35 formulas, mostly tonics created to support wellness.

She spent time exploring earth-based technologies before building a high desert greenhouse to grow her own food and herbs. The greenhouse is another step in her holistic vision and herbal work that includes saving seeds, planting, harvesting, making medicines. Cathy does phone consultations and collaborates with several holistic practitioners.

Cathy gladly shares with others these concepts of "growing in harmony." She now takes orders on a toll-free number and has a website.

Contact information

Cathy Hope
Iris Herbal Products
HC 81 Box 640
Questa, NM 87556
(505) 586-1802
Toll free: (877) 286-2970
website: www.irisherbal.com

Martha Oakes
Ayurvedic Postpartum Care

I educate the new mother so she knows she deserves to be taken care of, that she deserves a really deep recovery period because this is what nature wants of her.

This is my favorite rice recipe – Fancy Lemon Rice," said Martha Oakes, as I savored the colorful dish of basmati rice, raisins, red bell pepper, turmeric and lemon juice. Cooled by early June breezes, we sat on her front porch eating lunch – a lunch she had prepared and delivered to one of her clients before I arrived at her Boulder, Colorado, home. The yummy meal also featured steamed zucchini, sweet potatoes and Swiss chard sautéed in olive oil with ginger, tarragon and lemon juice, and a soup of French lentils, eggplant and seasonings.

Cooking is just one of the services Martha offers clients through her business, NewMother Ways, which provides postpartum care for mothers and babies. The 46-year-old's passion for mothering and motherhood can be seen in her gentle demeanor and the enlightenment she brings to her work.

Martha's education programs and home-care services are based on Ayurvedic principles that address this special time in a woman's life, a time when she is fragile. It is something that Western medicine overlooks, she said.

The knowledge and wisdom Martha shares with women stem from her longtime interest in spiritual and holistic practices. She has studied herbology, midwifery, Ayurveda and Transcendental Meditation. She received postpartum training at the Maharishi Ayurveda Medical Clinic in Fairfield, Iowa, and bore two of her three children at home.

"This program fills a gap in modern obstetrics and

natural childbirth practices, which generally emphasize only pregnancy, labor and delivery," Martha writes in her training manual, "NewMother Ways Parents' Handbook." "Ayurveda offers the missing understanding for restoring that natural balance which spontaneously generates good mothering. Simple protocols applied at this most delicate time have long-lasting influences. Mothers' experiences with their infants include less colic and early childhood sickness. Even more important, mothers find that they can recover much more quickly from the fatigue of pregnancy and delivery and can devote more love and attention to their children."

Ayurveda means "knowledge of life or daily living" and is derived from the Sanskrit words, ayus (life or longevity), and veda (knowledge or science). Ayurveda originated in ancient India approximately 5,000 years ago, and began celebrating a worldwide revival in the early 1980s through Maharishi Mahesh Yogi, founder of Transcendental Meditation and one of Martha's teachers.

The system is based on the five elements – earth, water, fire, air and ether (space) – and the manner in which the elements are uniquely balanced in each person. The five elements combine to create three basic constitutions or body types called doshas, which are kept in check through diet and exercise in relation to daily and seasonal influences.

Vata, the dosha that controls movement, is increased during childbirth, which is why women need special postpartum care, Martha said. "Birthing involves a great deal of bodily movement and change. The downward movement of all energies with the expulsion of a newborn draws energy from brain cells on downward and tends to greatly diminish the digestive power in the process."

The meals Martha prepares for her home-care clients and the recipes she provides nurture and support the postpartum digestive system. Excess Vata energy affects both physical and mental functions, and produces symptoms such as coldness, dryness, indigestion and gas, spaciness, anxiety, depression and insomnia. Foods need to be cooked and gently seasoned with herbs and spices that enhance digestion.

"The fundamentals of treatment are warmth, simplicity, oiliness, moisture, seclusion and of course, rest," she said. "It's real basic. You apply that to the massage, which is very gentle and simple. You use extra oil, it's warm; the room is extra warm. And you apply that to the diet. The mother is taking in extra oiliness, including clarified butter, throughout the day – adding it to a cup of hot milk, putting it in her soup and rice. She's cooking her rice with extra moisture, eating more soups, nothing raw or cold except sweet, fresh fruits."

Statistics show high incidence of blues, depression and psychosis among postpartum mothers, Martha noted. "Those are characteristics of Vata dosha imbalances. The body doesn't easily ground (itself in the face of) a lot of change at this time. It's very frustrating and gets to be depressing and deranging if it's not dealt with. But I seldom have women with blues. It's wonderful how much can be addressed so easily through taking care of her body, which takes the burden off the mom on the level of mind and emotions."

Martha knows well the strains of postpartum recovery and the benefits of Ayurvedic postpartum care. Her first marriage ended five weeks after her second child was born. And the care she received after the home birth of her third child at 38 was vital to regaining her health. "I didn't have any complications, but it was not an easy pregnancy or birth. It was really important that I had that help then.

"India isn't the only culture that has a history of addressing the special needs of postpartum women. Chinese, Colombian, Hispanic and Native American cultures, for example, historically have provided a reclusive healing time for new mothers. During this time, family members or doulas – mother helpers – perform many duties, such as cooking, house cleaning, shopping, child care and mother-baby massage. Some postpartum traditions indicate a 10- to 42-day recovery period; Ayurvedic tradition recognizes a special six-week, biological window for recovery," Martha said.

This six-week period is called kayakalpa or body time. It provides an opportunity for expanded consciousness and improved health because of the woman's unique body-mind state. Ayurveda believes kayakalpa occurs three times during a woman's life – marriage, postpartum and menopause. "It's nature's program," Martha said, "when the physiology is in a rare state of openness, when you can heal things you couldn't get at even before a previous pregnancy. It's a very sacred time."

This state of openness is also why a postpartum mother needs special care. "She's as fragile psycho-physiologically as a baby, but her heart is so open that she will want to say yes to everything that comes along. She needs to be mothered – educated and mothered." And that's just what Martha does, "leaving lots of room for creativity." She begins working with women before they have their babies so they'll have their support systems in place.

"I educate the new mother so she knows she deserves to be taken care of, that she deserves a really deep recovery period because this is what nature wants of her. I educate the husband, too, to understand that, yes, his wife may seem really different those weeks after the baby is born and it may be frightening to him that she doesn't have the attention for him, and her physiology and awareness are so different. But once he understands kayakalpa, that it's a special time and that it's not going to go on forever, he naturally learns to help her recovery process."

In her home-care program, Martha focuses mostly on the mom, although she monitors the baby's digestion and teaches moms how to do baby massage. This focus is different from the doula's role of helping around the house and tending baby. In addition to daily massage and cooking, Martha offers aromatherapy specific for postpartum needs, including women who have had difficult deliveries. She also uses herbal food supplements that aid digestion, lactation and help knit body tissues back together, and provides emotional support as needed. Her mother's manual holds a wealth of information about postpartum do's and do not's, menu suggestions and recipes, lists of Ayurvedic herbs, and how to give mother and baby massage. And when she needs information or sees red flags in a client's condition, Martha consults two local doctors she works with or recommends that the client see her own doctor.

Martha's journey into mother-baby work began in Fairfield, Iowa, around 1988 with the encouragement of her father, a doctor, and her mother, a registered nurse. Martha had been studying herbology for a year through the counsel of a Vedic (Ayurvedic) astrologer. She sent her father an herbal remedy for Christmas one year. He didn't care for the remedy, but he called her two weeks later after watching a program on midwifery and said he thought she'd make a great midwife. "So I thought, hmmmm. What a great bridge, and my folks are even encouraging me."

Midwifery became her passion. But after four months into a midwifery program, she sensed her need to balance midwifery with Ayurvedic postpartum health care. The latter had been introduced to the Fairfield community at the Maharishi Ayurveda Medical Center. Martha meditated, asked for guidance and got her answer the next day when Maharishi announced that he was offering a meditation course for professionals at Fairfield's Maharishi International University. Her decision to take the meditation course derailed her midwifery studies but enhanced her Ayurvedic studies. A year later, when her youngest son was 4, Martha studied postpartum massage at the medical center, returning her focus to mother-baby work.

"Maharishi just made it all available," Martha said about her years of Ayurvedic studies in Fairfield. "What draws me to it is the simplicity of it. When you talk about the elements to some people, it seems real abstract and esoteric at first. But we all know what hot and cold is, what moist and dry is, oily and smooth, settled and quiet. It's all so easily translatable to our life situations."

Since moving to Boulder in 1994, Martha has continued to study Ayurveda and to share her knowledge with women in public and private settings. (She is divorced now and shares the responsibility of raising her youngest son with his father in Iowa.)

"I work with women as much as possible and especially emphasize the theme of community. I heard recently that Hillary Clinton has written a book called `It Takes a Village.' I just love the title, because it really does take a village. You can't satisfactorily raise a child without acknowledging your village and working with it. That's my life challenge right now – working with my son and finding my village."

Martha also wants to teach more, to continue bringing light to the void in postpartum care. And she wants to pick up the threads of her midwifery career. "I'm still not a midwife, but I think I will be someday. My desire is to be simple, and these callings have their own timing. I like to have my hands in the earth, be in the garden. I want to be outside more, spend more time with my children. It's still a frustration that I haven't realized all those things. But my life is moving in that direction."

Healer update

Martha Oakes teaches a 150-hour certification and training program for Ayurvedic postpartum doulas. She no longer offers her personal services as a doula.

Martha added essential oils to her postpartum work and does healing sessions with her companion, who is an intuitive healer. She lives in California.

Contact information

Martha Oakes
Ayurvedic Doula and Postpartum Educator
NewMother Ways
email: martha@sacredwindow.com
(866) 224-0609

Martha's book, "NewMother Ways," can be purchased through Rocky Mountain Institute of Yoga and Ayurveda, P.O. Box 1091, Boulder, CO 80306; (303) 443-6923. Cost is $25, shipping and handling included. Send check only.

PART THREE

BODYWORKERS

Sister Elaine Pacheco
Social Worker/Massage Therapist

*T*his is a heightened time to be teaching and sharing what one knows. It's a time for awakening — for awakening what's already there, to discover the treasures within that the trauma of the past has dulled or hidden.

A black-and-white photograph lies atop a small stack of papers and folders on the floor next to Sister Elaine Lopez Pacheco. The photo, Sister Elaine explained, was taken when she was 3 years old, and her father carried it in his wallet for four decades until he died a few years ago. A special photograph, a special man. Her father was one of her first teachers in matters of the heart and more recently of letting go. He also was the reason why Sister Elaine returned to her hometown of Pueblo, Colorado, in 1983 after many years of working with impoverished people in the United States and abroad.

Sister Elaine's strong sense of service to family and community began with her large extended family of Hispanic heritage rooted in Northern New Mexico. Although she grew up in Pueblo, her family spent every summer of her youth in New Mexico. "I think that really affected me, became such a part of me – the land, my family, my love for the Hispanic culture," she recalled. "As the first-born in my family, I always had that sense of being loved, respected, honored. It just grew in me, became part of me. I tried to remain really true to my sense of place and to the region, its expansiveness of land. I feel that same kind of expansiveness is in oneself. And so knowing that as a young child, I learned to believe and honor that, learned to trust where that sense of spirituality would take me."

Since 1969, Sister Elaine has belonged to The Institute for the Sisters of Mercy of the Americas, an order of Roman Catholic nuns. She is a social worker and a bodyworker by profession, known for her compassionate ways, admired – and sometimes challenged – for her openness and progressiveness. "My family believed in the respect for other people and a sense of social justice; caring for other people and being compassionate. I am a Sister of Mercy; the true meaning of mercy is an enduring love. I can see that in my family. We've been connected and managed to stay connected. It's a gift, but it's also a skill."

There is a softness and gentleness about this woman of small stature. She speaks deliberately and reflectively about her life's work, punctuating her story with words like "giving" and "receiving," "connectedness" and "community," "co-creation" and "expansiveness." She fills her home environment with the simplicity and spaciousness she seeks in the landscapes of Southern Colorado, Northern New Mexico and Northern Utah, where she lived for eight years among the Northern Ute Indians. On this snowy April morning, we are warmed by the dancing flames in her fireplace as we sit side by side in the only two chairs in her living room. Stylish simplicity.

"My own spirituality had its beginnings in seeing that there was much more than just the narrow little nugget of organized religion," Sister Elaine said. Influenced by the movements of the 1960s, she embraced "not new, but original" concepts that viewed the "whole order of the universe." She studied sociology, which provided "a base of looking at the whole instead of parts," and she explored Eastern religions. "The '60s for me was a real emergence of ecumenism. Vatican II was in 1965. Religious orders – especially women's religious orders – took very seriously the changes. We did a lot of reading, talking and action, and we welcomed theologians who had new ideas. Theology was very expansive at that time."

Over the years, Sister Elaine has kept her global approach to religion and spirituality, welcoming concepts such as creation, spirituality, cosmology and quantum physics, and authors like Matthew Fox and Clarissa Pinkola Estes. But her most important "piece" is her practice of reflection and meditation. "For me it just continues to be a journey deeper and deeper into myself to what I already know. It's the same reality I had as a child, I'm just expanding it more. There haven't been certain goals, just staying true to being on that road, using the skills and intuition and opportunities that come to me."

Sister Elaine's path has not led to work within the Catholic Church, but it also has not distanced her from the Sisters of Mercy's mission and vision. "I felt my talents were best used outside my community-sponsored institutions. My work has always been with poor, indigenous people, which is one of our missions. It was an easy fit with being a social worker," she said. And her opportunities for service have been many, ranging from working in Mexican-American labor camps and Head Start programs to a brief stay in Nicaragua through Witness for Peace, where she was able to experience "the injustice that was happening by our country

supplying military machinery into Central America."
Before returning to Pueblo, she lived on Ute land in
Northern Utah where mentors were an Indian woman
named Violet Star and Dane Packard, a feminist minister
from the Berkeley, California, area.

She viewed her stay in Utah as a time to tend
"the seeds of receiving" that were planted by the Native
American movement in the '60s through her generation
(she is 46). Sister Elaine said her experience was a
deepening of all the things she knew and had practiced.
"It was another piece of being whole. My roots are in
Christianity, but I see it as only one foundation piece.
Through Violet – and the Native American spirituality
specific to the Northern Utes – I began to feel on a
different level. I've always been reflective, so I didn't
learn to be reflective. I learned to sit longer in the
silence." She also learned new ways to honor the land
and communicate with nature.

In keeping with her rhythm of giving and
receiving, Sister Elaine returned to Pueblo to be with her
family during her father's lengthy bout of Alzheimer's
disease. "It was another time to give back to my family
what they had done for me," she recalled. Her father
lost his voice during the early phase of his 12-year illness,
which "moved me again into a non-verbal world in
ways to communicate." It also provided new challenges.
"One of the things the disease offered me was more
reflection about alternative or non-accepted ways of
healing. I think all the other parts of my life were about
healing but in a different way."

That reflection led Sister Elaine to study the basics of Western massage (such as Swedish massage) and more recently Chinese massage or Tui-na (pronounced twee-na) at the New Mexico School of Healing Arts in Santa Fe. Combining her skills in social work with bodywork, she said, "was part of the journey back to Taoism through seeing energy and knowing what it is: That it is not just calories, that it is in all of us, that it is everywhere. Tui-na, basically, is energy work, knowing and understanding the function of the organs and the meridians; moving the energy by holding acupressure points and doing joint work so that healing can take place."

She uses touch and intuition "to communicate with people on an unconscious level. I 'talk' to them," she said, "and say 'You can do that, you can let go,' and it gives them hope. It tells them that there is more than institutionalized religion, more than the challenged family, more than the traumatized body. They're caught up in that and are looking for bridges. In my own way I am that kind of a bridge for many people." Sister Elaine serves as a bridge to other avenues of healing by referring clients to a variety of alternative health practitioners. She currently is learning about Chinese herbs and flower essences and – inspired by Violet Star's teachings on ceremonial herbs – is rediscovering her family's use of regional herbs for healing.

"I see that healing is just a lifelong journey, not something new or new to me. I'm a pretty pensive person and have always liked that part about me. It helps in the work place when you can step back from a situation, be reflective and see the whole. Now I use it in a broader text with quantum physics, knowing that we need the chaos, that we look at it, know that it is energy and that it holds information.

"I've always been very healthy, so when I started doing my own healing it wasn't because I was sick. We're at a very transformative time in the universe, and I want my body to be able to take all of this in. It's a time for awakening – for awakening what's already there, to discover the treasures within that the trauma of the past has dulled or hidden. The body is very important. We take it for granted, act like it doesn't exist. The puritanical belief system is alive and well and is killing us, so we need to learn how to honor the body."

"This wisdom is not new," Sister Elaine continued to emphasize, "but a return to love, trust, compassion and holism in a world where an oppressive, male-dominated hierarchy has prevailed. Seeing the need for the realignment in major institutions – family, government, religion – is not scary to me. It fits into the whole thing of chaos, the need to break up, renew and redefine." She referred to a "grid" co-created by the Sisters of Mercy: Awaken, Remember, Re-member, Co-create, Proceed. It's a process she currently is committed to as she helps her order redefine its actions on the eve of a new millennium.

"The question today is: What do we need to do to have meaning within institutional church? For me, it's using intuition. We're looking at a very patriarchal, hierarchical structure where women were not honored. In order to survive, I ask the same questions our founder did 170 years ago: What do we need to do for our work to continue? What effect does this work have on a social level, and what kind of message are we giving to society? Sisters of Mercy always have asked some hard questions of ourselves, and we're at a very crucial time to raise those questions again. Transforming from the old paradigm into the new, or returning to the origins of what a group of people can do, calls upon using your head, your heart and your body. And it means working co-creatively so that everyone makes it happen together; there is a mutuality from the beginning."

Sister Elaine admits that her approach – her openness – to change and experimentation through the co-creative process is being met with some resistance within the order. But she views the chaos as a necessary part of the process and is deeply committed to her community's growth. "In the future, one of the things that has been said (prophesies) is that we need to do things in groups, in communities. One thing the Sisters of Mercy has enhanced in me is that continuity of how you belong and how you make it work. It's all about preparation for me, in every aspect of my life. Preparation is more important than the main event."

Her father's death was about preparation, as well. "Diseases are our teachers. What my dad taught me was how to let go, not to stay feeling sad and to live that. My family was very lucky, had everyday lessons in

letting go. My dad put every other question in line –
life, death and rebirth, it was all there." His illness also
prepared her for the part-time work she does for the
local Alzheimer's disease association and returned her to
the neighborhood and the culture of her youth. And it
enables her to have a sense of place and "to remain with
mind, heart and body," she said.

Sister Elaine doesn't know how long she will stay
in Pueblo. Opportunities always come when she opens
to them, she said. "Some say that I'm risky; I see it as
being myself. There's no romanticizing it. My life hasn't
been focused on 'getting' a family but on extending
it out to a variety of people of different cultures in
different parts of the world. That is community. The
network is just tremendous."

Healer update

Sister Elaine Pacheco lived in Costa Rica for a while. Since her return to Pueblo, she has helped groups to restructure their organizations based on ecological principles. Sister Elaine is especially interested in working with women's groups, guiding women to their "own inner beings."

She still does healing work with individuals and has a special interest in the mentally ill.

Contact information

Sister Elaine Pacheco
Licensed Social Worker
Licensed Massage Therapist
Pueblo, CO
email: epach@pcisys.net

Heidi Wilson
Shiatsu Practitioner/Qui Dance
and Tai Chi Teacher

I feel that my purpose is to transform the mundane into something more alive. That's what my experience with dance and music was about, and it's the same with the healing work I do – to be part of changing energy.

Heidi Wilson knelt beside me as I lay on a futon in her office at Kwan Yin Center for the Healing Arts in Tucson, Arizona. I closed my eyes, surrendered my weight onto the futon and focused on my breath. Heidi placed one hand on my lower back, the other at the top of my left thigh. I could feel the gentle rocking motion of her body as she slowly fingered and palmed down my legs, up my torso and into my arms, tracing the meridians or energy pathways that needed balancing on that day. Heidi was doing Shiatsu, a form of Japanese bodywork that balances the flow of energy through the body and promotes healing. The session lasted for about an hour, and afterward I felt rested and more present.

In addition to her private practice at the Kwan Yin Center, Heidi teaches Shiatsu and qi dance at the Desert Institute of the Healing Arts in Tucson. It was this combination of Oriental healing arts and movement that piqued my interest in Heidi, along with her extensive background in the performing arts. I knew I had found an artist the night before when I watched Heidi lead a Shiatsu class in qi dance – her own form of dancing with qi or energy. Heidi moved with grace and a soft, meditative quality – similar to that of Taiji (Tai Chi) – while maintaining an awareness of her body and a connection to her surroundings. I watched her dance with energy in class; I felt her dance with energy when she did Shiatsu on me.

"There is no separation between the two," Heidi said. "I feel that my purpose is to transform the mundane into something more alive. That's what my exerience with dance and music was about, and it's the same with the healing work that I do – to be a part of changing energy."

Heidi's relationship with qi (also spelled chi or ki) has evolved over many years of creative practice. It began nearly 20 years ago after she moved from the Northeast to the Southwest to study dance at the University of Arizona at Tucson. She had heard a lot about Taiji (pronounced tie-gee) but didn't experience it until a dance instructor at the university required students who were learning a new piece of choreography to take Taiji classes. Heidi described Taiji as an ancient Chinese form of movement meditation that also is a healing art and a martial art. It integrates the mind, qi and the body. "I was the only one out of all the dancers to actually learn the whole Taiji form in the two months we had to learn it," Heidi recalled. "It just became part of me, and I felt aligned when I did it, when I tuned into the qi, the flow of the qi. I began to do Taiji just to feel united with the universe."

Heidi stands about 5-foot-3 and is lean and muscular. Her presence is commanding because of the space she uses when she moves and the energy she projects. She speaks in a low tone with words that are as deliberate and meditative as her dance movements. It seems like her outward expression is an extension of her peaceful inner landscape.

"Qi is an animated force, a life force, of the universe," Heidi said. "People translate it in many ways. It's very spiritual for me. God is energy in our bodies, and when we open our bodies to it we can have perfect health. It's limitless. It's really a matter of us tuning into it and not getting in its way. That's what I try to do when I teach. I'll tune into where different people's tensions are and try to get them to feel it. Then I figure out ways to work them through it so they can be on their own with it. I used to think that having them tune into their bodies was enough, but if they haven't had a lot of experience or tend to get stuck in their heads, they need to be guided through."

Sometimes when students are being too mental with their dance movements, Heidi asks them to jump up, run around the room and roll on the floor before resuming. This helps students to feel energy in their bodies. "To see them tune into the way their own spirits want to move and to be able to follow through is one of the most enjoyable and healing experiences that a teacher can have. When I was learning to be more in touch with my own center, my movement sense, I would go to a dance studio by myself, lay on the floor, wait for the movement to happen and go with it. I spent a summer doing that almost every day. So many people, even professional dancers, don't get to that place. They just think they need to go to class all the time and have somebody else show them what to do. Dance is about joy of movement and going with the flow, not standing tall and holding your leg up."

Experiencing joy in movement has come naturally to Heidi, who did a lot of imaginative, free play with friends and her three older sisters while growing up in the outdoors of New Haven, Connecticut. Her childhood dance teacher was one of the original members of Doris Humphrey's modern dance company, and she encouraged natural dance through endless combinations of leaps, falls and turns. Heidi began playing the oboe at age 12 (she switched to the saxophone at 19) and studied classical music with the encouragement of her parents, who both were classical musicians. But she eventually convinced her instructor to let her improvise the music and later studied improvisational jazz. Perhaps because she was the youngest child, Heidi rebelled the most against her family's conventions. She spent a lot of time alone in the woods when she was 15 and 16 communicating with insects and birds and having visions about creation. She also became a vegetarian at this time.

Heidi's urge to go somewhere she hadn't been before took her to Tucson. Before she completed her dance studies at the university, she met a drummer and poet who was her companion for many years and later fathered her two daughters. The couple started doing concerts combining creative music, dance and poetry. "It was strong, expressive, original stuff – experiential. A lot of times, we studied traditional jazz standards rooted in black music," Heidi said. "Then when I started combining the music, dance and poetry in the group we had, the dance was very much Taiji. It varied in rhythms, but always was rooted in trance with one movement flowing out of another. That's when I started developing the idea of Qi Dance. I was teaching dance and Taiji separately, then started putting them together. Then I found a new Taiji teacher and learned to do the form more correctly. I kept practicing, all the while teaching Qi Dance as a freer form."

While Heidi continued to expand her knowledge of Taiji, she also learned two other Chinese internal and martial arts – Pa Gua and H'sing-I. "All three forms are part of Qi Gong, which is the art of breathing, energy control and movement. Qi Gong is not a martial art, but Taiji, Pa Gua and H'sing-I initially were used to increase the body's internal physical strength for combat. They also proved to be effective in healing the body and prolonging life and are gentler when practiced without the martial arts component. Taiji is the slowest and softest of the three," she explained. "Pa Gua is very powerful, is rooting and grounding and deals more in spirals, working in circles. H'sing-I is faster. I've heard it described as dealing more with lightning. The movements in each of the forms represent the different qualities of the five elements of Chinese medicine – earth, fire, water, wood, metal – and healing to the internal organs. Traditional Qi Gong exercises are good for aligning the spine and strengthening the legs so the qi can go from the belly down to the earth and open up to the heaven energy through the upper body. The result is a feeling of centeredness."

Qi Gong also helped Heidi to create movement in her personal life and led her to Shiatsu. She didn't know much about Shiatsu, other than that it was energy work, when she started thinking about going to massage school several years ago. She felt called to do healing work and followed her heart by enrolling in the Desert Institute for the Healing Arts' Shiatsu program (the school also offers a year-long course in massage therapy). She completed the program three years ago. "It was a very natural evolution from being involved with music and dance to doing bodywork. I really made the connection to energy when I learned Shiatsu. I had studied Taiji all these years, practiced it and taught it, created Qi Dance. But when I made contact with another person's energy, that's when I started making connections in Taiji. That's when it all made sense. My body wasn't constricting anything and really started to respond to energy."

The Shiatsu school asked Heidi to teach after she graduated. She felt like she needed more experience before teaching Shiatsu, but offered to enhance the school's curriculum with Qi Dance. She co-taught Shiatsu technique for the first time in spring 1995. The school follows the teachings of Shizuto Masunaga of Japan who developed his technique in the early 1900s from ancient Chinese acupuncture theories. Acupuncture uses needles in isolated points to stimulate or regulate energy flow to weak or over-active organs, while Shiatsu practitioners work the entire body with manual manipulation and joint stretches. "Shiatsu is more about tuning into the energy of the meridian and finding tsubos (acupuncture points) that are just there," Heidi explained. "This is where you get access to the energy. You're not depending on just one point to move the energy or memorizing where the point is, although we do study where traditional points are. With Shiatsu you tend to find places along the meridian that give you access to the energy and open up the whole body to it."

Some of Heidi's clients are referred by acupuncturists at the Kwan Yin Center, which is named after the Chinese goddess of compassion and mercy. Shiatsu and acupuncture are complementary therapies, she said. "Some of the referrals have chronic ailments, and Shiatsu opens them up for the acupuncture. Other clients come for different reasons, for maintenance, which helps to keep them open to their energy and to strengthen their immune system." Fibromyalgia responds really well to Shiatsu, she said, as well as menstrual problems and a condition called "restless legs," common in older women.

But just a small percentage of the American public really knows about Shiatsu's healing benefits, and it will take time to educate people about Shiatsu, Heidi said. Even Shiatsu students discover there is more to this healing art than just theory. "It really takes more than a year to be able to tune into the qi. You have to stay present, to keep total focus. Shiatsu addresses the whole person. Each organ and system is associated with an emotion as well as a physical and mental function. It is taught that Shiatsu opens up the energy and balances our whole being through this integrated system. But there's another dimension that I'm beginning to discover.

"I just completed a course in Reiki II, so I know the energy just isn't in the body. It comes in from the universe, from the higher power, and it's a matter of opening the body up to receive it. That's part of my dilemma of teaching it in school because the program is so theory based. I like to just go to the meridian that needs work, find and open up the tsubo, send energy to the place in the person that needs the change, and it will happen. Adding your intention and images can be really helpful. That's what I try to tune into, not to get too hung up on the mental aspect of manipulating the energy. It's more about observing, being present, sensing where the energy needs to go and having compassion."

Heidi's knowledge and gifts are many and include the practice of Hatha Yoga and meditation. She considers her greatest gift to be compassion with balance, which is fitting for this Libra woman. "My upbringing with music and dance was leading me to use all of that movement and beauty to heal. I really feel the performing arts are healing arts, too. I feel I'm more in service this way, although I'm not through with performing." Living her life in purpose has brought Heidi in touch with others who are doing the same. "I seem to be connecting with people who have faith in something beyond the pain that people are in right now, who know what it is that we're a part of. It's an awareness of some better times coming." And Heidi is committed to being part of that changing energy.

Healer update

Heidi Wilson continues to practice and teach her healing arts. Her practice includes a new form of Cranio-Sacral therapy – Visionary Cranio-Sacral Work.

Contact information

Heidi Wilson
1032 E. King St.
Tucson, AZ 85719
(520) 888-4780
email: heidiwc8@aol.com

Pamela Machutt
Practitioner of Developmental Movement/
BodyMind - Centering

Most of the children I
work with have experienced birth
trauma, being born two to three
months early. The way I work
is very successful, and these
children come a long way pretty
quick. In a year's time, they
can be crawling, sitting, talking —
things the medical profession said
they would never do.

P amela Machutt lives in the desert just west of Tucson, Arizona, with rattlesnakes, scorpions, tarantulas and black widows. She talks casually about the rattlesnake that recently began seeking respite from June's three-digit temperatures in a corner of her carport.

Pamela feels comfortable living in the desert and seems to view it as a necessity rather than a risk. Whether in the wilds of rural Minnesota where she grew up or in the untamed desert, she always has thrived in nature and drawn energy from it. She calls it gathering energy. "I knew what gathering energy was from a young age. I could feel when I needed to gather energy or to express energy. I experience the energy in many, many ways, in all forms, both plant and animal."

This ability to sense and direct energy is one of many gifts Pamela brings to her work as a practitioner of Body-Mind Centering and CranioSacral Therapy. Pamela also integrates numerous other therapies into her work, which has evolved from two decades of study and experience.

"It's hard to say in a nutshell what I do because I do so many different things," she said. "Essentially I'm bringing together 20 years of movement and movement therapy training and experience as a dancer, as a movement therapist, as a choreographer, as a performer, as a teacher, as a healer and as a student."

To understand the scope of Pamela's work, I participated in a class she taught on developmental movement – one aspect of Body-Mind Centering – at the University of Arizona in Tucson. I also observed a private session during which she worked with an 18-month-old girl who was born prematurely, has cerebral palsy and seizures. As I watched her teach and work, I clearly saw the natural progression of dancer to therapist. Dance and Body-Mind Centering (BMC) have a common thread: movement.

BMC is an experiential study of anatomical, physiological and developmental principles that uses movement, touch, sound and guided imagery. Clients are actively engaged in discovering their bodies – from bones to soft tissues to organs to blood – and learn how to integrate all these parts through movement and healing touch. Movement re-education and hands-on repatterning are considered important keys to a client's healing process and can change limiting movement patterns and enhance perceptual-motor development.

Pamela studied BMC with its founder, Bonnie Bainbridge Cohen, who has studied the body-mind connection for more than 35 years. Certification takes about four years.

When I entered the university gymnasium to observe Pamela's developmental movement class, I saw Pamela the dancer and teacher. She was sitting off to the side, momentarily looking at notes and preparing for the morning's work. Pamela stood and walked to the center of the room; her loose-fitting top and pants rippled gently against her tall, well-toned and tanned body. Her eyes were vibrant, her smile warm as she gathered her students into a circle and continued her talk from the previous day about the body's 12 neurological patterns and the evolution and quality of each pattern. The three-week intensive course just skims the surface of available material, Pamela said. "I've been studying this since 1979, and I feel like I know three-quarters of it. It's one of those things that's never-ending."

The class was mostly experiential. We explored some of the neurological patterns and the feelings they evoke through subtle movements in seated and standing positions and more physical, crawling movements on the floor. They all felt reptilian. We also used various sizes of large balls to explore more expansive movements on a rolling surface. It was fun but not easy, and the gym resounded with grunts, groans and outbursts of laughter. Each pattern is supported by primitive reflexes, righting reactions (which allow one to remain upright) and equilibrium responses. All provide the foundation for efficient adult movement.

Children who suffer birth trauma and brain injury, like Pamela's infant clients, miss pieces of the developmental sequence, but through emotional healing and hands-on repatterning can learn to integrate the missing pieces. Pamela showed me how this happens as she worked with her infant client with cerebral palsy in her home later that afternoon. She used some of the re-patterning movements I had experienced in class. She placed one hand at the base of Abbey's spine and her other hand at the crown of the infant's head. Pressing gently against the two extremities or end points, Pamela slowly followed Abbey's movement. First Abbey's head and pelvis curled inward, paused, then she slowly arched her head back. Pamela repeated the spinal movements for about 15 or 20 minutes, while she mimicked Abbey's wails and aligned and massaged her arms. She took short breaks when Abbey's crying or coughing required comforting by her mother. Abbey was on the floor during the second half of the session in a crawling position. Pamela continued to use touch and sound to stimulate and connect with Abbey, added colorful toys for her to look at, and tried a range of crawling postures with her legs. After the session, Pamela said how much Abbey had benefited from just a few months of therapy and that she eventually will be able to sit, crawl, walk and talk.

"Developmental movement is this: Think of one thing that links every human on Earth, no matter where they were born or how they were brought up, what their genes are. It's that we all go through the same movement patterns from the time we are conceived to about two years of age, and you'll see the complete cycle in normal development. That holds true into other mammals, reptiles, amphibians, fish. There's a set hierarchy, and everybody will pass through the sequence in some form. They may skip something, which would be abnormal development, but the sequence is set."

Pamela's interest in movement started at age 20, when she watched her first dance performance at the college in her hometown of Winona, Minnesota. "I didn't come from a family that had any knowledge of the arts or performance arts," Pamela said. She had played musical instruments since she was a child and enjoyed popular dance but didn't know that one could study dance. The performance "just blew me away," she recalled. So the next day she enrolled in some dance classes and began working with musician friends to combine movement and music. Pamela's creative explorations drew her to Boulder, Colorado, where she studied dance at Naropa Institute and began a natural progression into body-mind therapies.

"There's the many years of background in different movement trainings and therapies, as well as in performance. I was a modern dancer for about 12 years, and I choreographed pretty much from the beginning. So I actually was doing more multi-media – incorporating dance, music, film, theater. All the while there was a strong interest in the body because I came into dance late. The art I knew before that was music, so I looked at the body as my instrument. From the very beginning, I was studying with people who were movement-based but were looking at the body in a very dynamic way and investigating it through hands-on work, as well as taking traditional physiology, kinesiology and anatomy and applying it to healthy, dynamic bodies."

Pamela's 12 years of dancing were coupled with the study of disciplines ranging from movement to martial arts to bodywork and non-traditional approaches to body-related sciences. She studied six hours a day, then worked six hours a day, constantly balancing her intuitive and analytical gifts. She studied bodywork methods like Shiatsu and Rolfing mostly with individuals, many of whom taught courses at Naropa. And the wide array of jobs she held connected her with many different people, including children and people in hospices and psychiatric institutions. Dance also provided some international travel opportunities to experience other cultures.

"I always was very independent, self-reliant and self-directed because of the family I grew up in. I went after what I wanted from a very young age. We didn't have money for extras, so when I wanted to take a trip somewhere because my other friends were doing it, I had to find some way to get the money. I'd always find something right away and was very successful at it. It took me into many walks of life. I've probably had about 300 different jobs in my life, sometimes five at one time. I always called them my subculture jobs."

In 1985, Pamela shifted her focus from performance to therapy. During the years that followed, she had many mentors who were accomplished and pioneering individuals, and she started her own private practice. She wasn't driven to learn, she said, but was stimulated to discover the pieces she needed. She became certified in infant massage, BMC, visceral (organ) massage and CranialSacral Therapy, which balances the flow of cerebrospinal fluid in the brain and spinal cord through light pressure. She studied Hakomi Bodywork (now called Hakomi Integrative Somatics), a body-centered psychotherapy; she developed a program for parents and infants based on play and psychomotor development. Through her involvement with the Pre- and Peri-Natal Psychology Congress of North America, she met and studied with the late Graham Farrant, an Australian psychologist who worked with cellular consciousness, and William Emerson, who works with people affected by pre-birth and birth traumas.

Ninety-five percent of Pamela's clients have been "written off" by Western medical traditions and practices, she explained. They are told either to have surgery or that nothing can be done. "Most of the children I work with have experienced birth trauma, being born two or three months early. The way I work is very successful, and these children come a long way pretty quick. In a year's time, they can be crawling, sitting, talking – things the medical profession said they would never do. I address both the trauma patterns and imprints. That's probably the most unique thing that I do. It's interesting that I've done and stayed with this for the longest period of time. It's not my only purpose, but it's a real central focus."

Pamela is often asked to help set up programs based on her expertise. She teaches workshops and Body-Mind Centering at the Desert Institute for the Healing Arts. "I've always been a teacher, starting at a pretty young age of 11 or 12 when I volunteered at a camp for developmentally delayed kids. Anything I ever studied, I taught – immediately. It helps me to integrate the material, move with it, develop it." Everything she learns, she learns by experiencing or living it. And things always have presented themselves at the right time. This has been especially true of her spiritual practices, which have included Tibetan Buddhism, Hinduism and Native American.

"I've always followed my feelings. It's kind of like what I get from nature, that gathering of energy when the energy just comes in and it just totally wakes me up. It comes in all different ways. Basically, it's kind of like I have this big bag of tricks that I can pull out if I want to, and sometimes I do. I think it's also that once you gather your bag of tricks, as time goes on you don't even carry the bag around any more, much less open it.

"Recently I've been looking at what my purpose is; asking what is my intention in this lifetime, what am I here for? My purpose through my work obviously is the discovery of self in relationship to other people, in relationship to service, in relationship to our true nature. My purpose is to bring the spirit into the body, so to speak.

"But what I do is constantly changing. I'm doing something that really hasn't been named. In my private practice, I never had an agenda. In teaching, I'm not using an agenda anymore either. Just going moment to moment. Sometimes I might do bodywork as a client and I are hiking. What I'm doing more and more is to spontaneously incorporate the environment, the outdoors. Last December I decided I was going to call this 'Eco-bodywork.' For me it's just much easier to connect through nature without any kind of judgment, without anything overlaying it. In nature the clarity of the spirit is much more present in form. Somehow I am

131

to bring in the weavings of the sacred work and the nature spirit – that incredible life force and beauty in all its clarity – and align it with the human body."

Healer update

Pamela Machutt spends time in Asia and has moved her home base to Northern California. She has a private practice and does some teaching, mostly in the Sacramento area.

Contact information

Pamela Machutt
P.O. Box 668
N. San Juan, CA 95960
(530) 292-1636

Soltahr
Reiki Master/Counselor

Yes, I am a witch.
To me it means that part of my
life is magic. It's how I bend
and shape my world.

When I arrived at Soltahr's home in Lafayette, Colorado, she was celebrating Brigid with some friends. "Today is a feast day," Soltahr said after her friends departed. "It's one of our Earth holidays. We're celebrating the midpoint between winter solstice and spring equinox. We're celebrating the quickening – things coming back to life."

Soltahr is a Pagan, a word that means people of the land or heath, country dwellers. Paganism is an ancient, nature-oriented religion that recognizes many gods and honors Mother Earth, her cycles and our relationships to them. "Essentially, the idea is recognizing the balance of things – the male and female, the god and goddess, yin and yang; that we all have each of those within us," Soltahr said. "It's the recognition of Earth as our mother, our nurturer and caretaker."

It is this connection to Earth that helps Soltahr balance her busy life as a Reiki practitioner and teacher, a student at Naropa Institute in Boulder, Colorado, and a single mother of 7-year-old twin daughters. And celebrating the quickening on this sunny mid-winter day gives her hope that spring and rebirth is on the way.

"This is my favorite time of year. I love the way trees have been barren, and then over a period of weeks the buds swell. That for me is where the magic is – that wondrous, continual process of ebb and flow, life and death, birth and rebirth, and recognizing our connection to that cycle. To me that's what Paganism is about, that celebration of that deep cycle within ourselves. That is what gives my life meaning, what has been the guiding force of my life. That connection gives me a lot of peace."

Soltahr also finds peace in the Zen practice of sitting meditation, which she learned last fall when she started working on a master's degree in transpersonal psychology at Naropa Institute. Sitting meditation is the practice of being in the present moment, where one learns how to quiet the mind by recognizing and releasing thoughts and focusing on the breath. "That practice has helped me to be right here, right now, and not worrying about the future," Soltahr said. "It's simple, and you're taken care of on some level. Because there's something about when you're on the right path, honoring your soul's purpose, trying your best to be right where you need to be, that everything seems to work out OK."

As sunlight streamed into her living room, Soltahr talked openly about her life's journey and the ongoing challenge of healing herself so she can better heal others. There is a gentleness about her when she speaks; her eyes smile as she smiles. Her dark brown skin is supple and radiant, belying her 42 years. Necklaces with a crystal, a goddess and other charms drape her chest; a band of silver bracelets chimes softly as she gestures. Her joy and her green outfit capture the spirit of this feast day, the coming of spring.

Soltahr hides little about herself because she is an honest and a big woman. Her lifestyle is simple and often meager, yet she always has what she needs. Her past relationships with men have not been healthy, she said, she has a history of overeating, the long days of juggling school with her healing practice and parenting are stressful. She's doing a lot of personal healing right now and that has its painful moments, she said. But she tempers the pain and stress by honoring who she is – a witch – and practicing her craft alone and with others.

"Yes, I am a witch," Soltahr said, "but I don't use the term very often. It tends to put people off, and there are a lot of misconceptions about witchcraft. To me it means that part of my life is magic. It's how I bend and shape my world." Ritual is the vehicle Soltahr uses to create magic, to "bend and shape" the subtle energies and nature spirits of the unseen world. Craft rituals can induce trance or altered states of awareness that enable participants to tap their inner powers, their intuition, and to connect with the world of spirit – the divine. Rituals can be used to heal, to bring insight and inspiration, to aid rebirth.

"Ordinary things done on a regular basis like brushing our teeth or preparing for the workday or the change of seasons also are rituals," Soltahr explained. "Rituals are ways to keep order; they are ways to bring the sacred into our daily lives. I've always used rituals as a way to improve myself," she said. "Seasonal ritual gives me more understanding of time and self. It helps to have more information about the seasons, the waxing and waning light so I can get more sunshine when I need it. Or to connect with the phases of the moon – to know when to bring in energy or to let go, when to be quiet or when to celebrate the fullness of what you have."

Soltahr often suggests ways that clients can deepen their healing process with rituals. Recently, during a new moon, Soltahr performed a ritual with a women's group which reflected the group's focus on self-improvement and self-healing. "We were dedicating ourselves as healers," Soltahr said. "We did things that would strengthen and heal us. We blessed our hands that we might heal, blessed our mouths that our words of wisdom might heal others."

Soltahr began doing healing work after she became a Pagan and realized that healing was to be her life's work. She used and taught others how to use rituals, herbs and crystals. She started healing with her hands about four years ago when she learned Reiki from a shaman and Reiki Master in her hometown of Colorado Springs, Colorado. When she completed the first level of classes, she experienced what she felt when she was introduced to Paganism. "It was a simple, strong feeling that I'd come home," Soltahr recalled. Through Reiki, she found another way to use energy to heal herself and others, another way to connect with the mysterious forces of the universe. Soltahr continued to study Reiki and received her mastership several years later. She also did a lot of personal healing during that time and got divorced. She attributes her shifts in awareness to Reiki and the non-traditional counseling she received.

"Reiki is a spiritually guided life force or energy," Soltahr explained. "This life force exists throughout the universe and is in everything around us – the Earth, the sun, the air, fire and water. There are lots of forms of energy in the Universe. The Universe is like a radio, and there's all kinds of radio stations. To tune into Reiki is tuning into that channel. Doing an attunement is simply opening up the vortex in your own body, being a receiver. You are then able to bring it through and give it to a person, and their body uses it as it will for its own healing."

New doors opened for Soltahr through Reiki. She began teaching Reiki and even did Reiki sessions at psychic fairs for a while. "Mostly it seems that my work has revolved more around the combination of teaching and healing – my chosen path. I strongly believe that my soul's purpose is to help others become healers. The neat thing about Reiki is that you can use it on yourself. I feel that more people need to learn how to heal themselves. Healing others is a good thing, but it's best to start here," she said, pointing to her heart.

Through the support of friends and her belief system, Soltahr moved with her daughters to the Boulder area last fall and started graduate studies at Naropa – a school she always had wanted to attend. She saw it as one more step along her path and an opportunity to deepen her counseling skills. "It was my first experience of jumping off the cliff," Soltahr laughed. "I jumped and said, 'OK Spirit, be my parachute, my net, my wings,' and watched amazing things happen."

Naropa's Buddhist-based teachings dovetailed well with Soltahr's beliefs and practices, and offered what she needed to enhance her work as a healer.

"What drew me to the program was the idea that everything is connected, that there is no separation of body, mind, spirit and emotion. Western medicine says there's drugs or surgery – that's all they offer you. Eastern thought and other approaches heal the whole being. Transpersonal psychology says, yes, they are connected. And it brings in that spiritual aspect that has long been left out of counseling."

Soltahr practiced these different approaches by working at a variety of counseling jobs in both traditional and non-traditional systems. She was a case manager for the department of social services. She worked at a battered women's shelter, where she realized that her counseling skills could enhance her work as a healer. She also worked at an abortion clinic, where women served women. Soltahr believes she did some of her most difficult but best work there. "It was really hard, but there was something about it – that feeling of helping other women to go through a very difficult experience, to make a difficult decision – that was wonderful. It was a very supportive atmosphere."

Women are Soltahr's favorite clients. Their issues and emotional wounds are one of the reasons why Soltahr went back to school. "As I did Reiki on people, things would come up – old patterns and workings. I didn't want them to leave the session with unfinished business." She also wanted to give clients more tools to heal themselves.

By helping others to learn more about themselves, Soltahr is challenged to practice what she knows. "The Zen concept for it is mindfulness," she said. "Zen teaches you how to deal with something as it comes up rather than slipping into old patterns or freaking out. You take a few breaths and look at it. My goal is to be aware of those patterns right when they happen and get back on track."

Soltahr considers her biggest test to be her daughters. They are the most challenging job of her life, she said. She wants to teach them to be mindful and responsible beings. She wants to use wisely the information available to her at this time, information that wasn't available to previous generations of parents. She recently began teaching them how to do rituals. "This is the time we've all been waiting for – to enlighten ourselves. The world consciousness is going to start moving in that direction. How to be more lively, in such a way that we get along with each other and the Earth."

Spiritual practices that are Earth-based. Recognizing the changing of seasons, seeing the beauty around us. Taking time to celebrate that beauty. Soltahr lights up with the possibilities. "All of this wonderful light is coming into our world. It's just flooding in, and we can just ride on that wave of bettering ourselves, bettering each other and bettering the Earth."

Healer update

Soltahr completed her master's degree in transpersonal psychology. She is academic advisor at Naropa University in Boulder, Colorado, where she also teaches diversity – how to make connections with all of humanity and all life.

Soltahr still does private healing work.

Contact information

Soltahr (Gail Sanford)
Soltahr – Healing Woman
Boulder, CO
home email: soltahr@earthnet.net
office email: gailsan@naropa.edu

PART FOUR

SHAMANS AND SPIRITUAL HEALERS

Diana Velazquez
Curandera

One of my purposes for being in a public place was to start opening doors and building bridges of communication between the professionals and the traditional healers. And it's been very successful.

Diana Velazquez props herself up with pillows and fidgets, trying to get comfortable. It is a workday in early May and she is resting at her Northern Colorado home (a rare occasion for this busy professional), recovering from a fall at work. "I slipped on my heel," Diana explained, then looked off into space. "I was being stupid and clumsy." But a few hours with this woman, whose mission in life was determined at birth, reveals that there are more accurate words to describe her. "Bright, bold, courageous" are ones I would choose.

Diana is director of Centro de las Familias, a mental health center in northwest Denver that serves Mexican and Spanish-speaking people. She also is coordinator for the handful of programs she supervises outside Centro de las Familias. Her credentials: curandera. "That must give you an idea of the kind of physicians who work with us," Diana said. "They don't feel threatened."

But it didn't begin that way. Diana kept silent about her healing gifts when she first took a secretarial position at the Denver mental health agency that specializes in Chicanos 20 years ago. "But being the quiet, shy, non-assertive Chicana that I am," Diana said with a laugh, "I couldn't keep my mouth quiet about treatments. We weren't looking at a complete picture in terms of spirituality." While taking notes on a particular case, she read that the social worker thought the patient was hexed. Diana became upset about the social worker's disregard for the patient's symptoms and shared her feelings with her boss. Her boss agreed to let her see the woman.

"I talked with her, recognized the symptoms, did what I needed to do. And she responded immediately – within 45 minutes. I talked her lingo. Someone finally was believing her, taking care of her. I gave her tools to do the work herself so she wouldn't have to be hospitalized again. She learned ritual for her protection." Diana's treatment changed the woman's life. And it changed her own.

"When I left the office that Friday I left as a secretary that was well-loved, efficient, charming," Diana recalled. "On Monday, I came back to where people didn't want to get near me and were real scared of me." When the center received 17 requests from people wanting "this kind of business" the following week, the director decided Diana's work would enhance their program and created a one-year trial position for her. "If it didn't go, I could return to my secretarial job. That's been 20 years ago. I guess it's going to work."

Today, Diana supervises a staff of social workers, psychiatrists, a nurse, psychiatric technicians – people with bachelor's and master's of arts degrees. She does therapy and healing sessions at the center and through her private practice (Anglos seek her out as well), but "It's hard to get an appointment with me," she said. Diana occasionally teaches seminars on curanderismo, and each week she gets calls from two or three "brain pickers" – students who want to interview her for school reports and research. "I think one of my purposes for being in a public place was to start opening doors

149

and building bridges of communication between the professionals and the traditional healers. And it's been very successful."

That's a brave undertaking for a woman who represents a long lineage of Hispanic healers who have had to conceal their practices from the Anglo community. "Fifty years ago you talked about a curandera and you got slapped into an institution. We haven't always been open and accepted," Diana said. "I had to be very secretive about what I did. I went to school, I came home. I was not allowed to get involved with friendships or after-school activities so I could keep my focus; so the gringos wouldn't find out about it and accuse me of being a witch or try to take me away from my family or the barrio. If the teachers knew that when I got home I went to see people, mixed herbs and rubbed eggs over people, said special ceremonies and was known to do magic, they would have seen this as ungodly and that I was being abused or neglected. I never did have any little friends or play. Now that I'm old, I get to do it – the friends, the play and the dolls. It was seen as something that was not needed. I'm sure that if my dad and grandmother in their infinite wisdom knew that I needed it they would have supplied it. But it's about prioritizing, what's important to your learning."

Diana's first teacher was her grandmother; her schoolroom was the barrio in San Antonio, Texas, where she was born. Her grandmother was considered a general practitioner or curandera total, a healer of the highest status who employs many healing methods. Her grandmother had expected her oldest, favored daughter to give birth to a child with healing gifts ("We're always daughters of daughters"), but it was her youngest daughter who bore the healer.

"Certain things need to happen while in your mother's womb. It's not only that your mother needs to hear the crying in the womb, it needs to be heard by someone else in the community. Then, at the time of your birth, there is always a curandera present to be sure that all the other signs are there. At my birth there was one curandera, but my grandmother also was there. She wanted her oldest daughter to be the one to have the healer in the family – which follows the normal process – and had trouble accepting that it was my mother instead. So she had to be there to be double sure. I was the blessed one, or cursed one, depending on how you look at it," Diana laughed.

Starting at an early age, Diana's grandmother taught her how to mix herbs, treat illnesses and do midwifery. "I was trained from the beginning to know everything. One of the benefits, I believe, of being trained as a child is that there are no barriers to tell you that you can't do something. They tell you that you're real bright so you believe it." Diana also believed that her father knew what was best for her, so she didn't question her arranged marriage to a Yaqui Indian at age 15. "I was told since I was quite young that I had a mission in life, that certain things during my life needed to happen in order to fulfill that mission. I was told that this was one of the things that needed to happen. And I know my father loved me very much and that he wouldn't do anything that would hurt me."

The teen-ager and her new husband moved to the Yaqui Indian reservation in Sonora, Mexico. There she continued to study healing practices with her husband's father, a Yaqui medicine man. "I tell people that I have my master's degree from Texas and my Ph.D. from the Indian reservation," Diana said. "It was really difficult for me, having been born in America and used to all the basics in life to have to go and live very, very primitively. Fortunately, I was young." There were obstacles. At that time, American-born women were viewed as weak and needy, she said. And there were language barriers: Diana's Spanish was "Spanglish," a mixture of English and Spanish that was different from the more "perfect" Spanish spoken by the Yaqui. "Nobody understood me in Mexico, so that has been one of my goals in life: To learn Spanish and learn it well. Which I did."

Diana lived with the Yaqui for six years, during which time she had two children. She and her family returned to San Antonio, where she practiced curanderismo for 10 years and nearly burned out. They moved to Denver, and the few months Diana spent as an unknown were the happiest times of her life. Then she felt called to return to community work.

"If you ask me, what do you do?" said Diana, "I teach you or help you to heal your wounded spirit. I see people with spiritual stuff, because anything that becomes emotional or mental, I really believe is spiritual. We live in an era, a time, when we don't nourish our spirits. So when we run out of fuel, then the rest of the system starts breaking down.

"Have things changed since my grandmother practiced? It's changed but it hasn't. It's changed in terms of names; it's gone from 'nuts' to 'crazy' to 'psychotic.' It's changed in terms of people disconnecting themselves from their heart and their spirit and working entirely in their head. I'm aware of that because I've had to do it – to connect my spiritual being with my mental thinking processes in order to do some of the things an administrator does. It can feel very empty. But people in general walk around without really ever connecting those parts of themselves. In terms of what I saw when I was much younger and what I see now, and I'm 55: I see a lot of robots today."

Diana encourages all of her clients to take responsibility for their lives, and in her private practice seldom sees the same client more than three times a year. "My goal is to give these people tools so they can take care of themselves. Sometimes it's hard for them to understand processing in a session. But there's something about what I do that makes people listen. They get a treatment, laying on of hands, cleansings, or they take a long list of things they need to do at home, such as candles to light and prayers to say at certain hours. I may recommend that they take herbs or baths with sacred salts that I make, or do rituals with the healing oils I make. Whatever it is, it starts their process. It feeds their soul."

This healer, who is "aware of time past, time present and time future," has many tools. "I use herbs, candles, oils, colors, nature, the moon, the sun, metals, alexandrite, my hands. If I have to say what is the one thing I would do out of everything, it would be the ritualistic part. I use a lot of rites and rituals for healing purposes, some that I learned from both cultures. But as I'm out there in the world, more and more it appears to me that there is somewhere inside me, like a little tiny computer chip, that when something is needed," she pauses and snaps her fingers, "the herb, ritual, where to touch, the treatment plan will come. I don't remember sitting and saying, you mix this and this and then you bring it together to mix this. My teaching was more about you don't mix these two herbs in the same pan, you don't put them in the same location, you don't pick them at noon, you pick them at night, and you don't pick the land dry. That's what I remember. The rest is just knowing exactly what to do. I just create it."

Although Diana's practice of curanderismo has become well accepted and respected in her community, she still feels pressure to perform. "I have to walk a very, very fine line, a tightrope. Someone has a pair of scissors over here ready to cut, and someone has a lighter over here ready to burn it down. And sometimes I feel walking in both worlds – spiritual and reality-based – that I have to come up with a miracle a month to keep my credibility. Nobody else has to do that."

Curanderismo has remained an active part of the

Hispanic community over the years, Diana said. "It's just that the old ones are dying or getting senile. The new ones never really took an active interest in learning, or there's not enough legitimate ones, meaning that if you have to advertise in a shopping mall that you're God's gift, then you're not any good. You either have it or you don't, and when you have a limited knowledge you can be very dangerous. I really don't believe that any one of us was put on Earth with one method to heal every single thing."

Curanderismo is a way of life for Diana. She has a special room at Centro de las Familias – "a peaceful place" – where clients can light candles and incense, where she can teach them rituals and chants, where she can do hands-on work on a massage table. "My father always said that God had a special thing for me, and this must be it because I love what I'm doing. I enjoy it and get paid for it."

As Diana walks me to her front door, she is quick to point to her other love: her family. There is the snapshot of her son-in-law and daughter, who assists Diana's clients when she is out of town. There is the snapshot of Diana's son at her side after she received an award of excellence from the University of Colorado for her accomplishments in the field of psychology. And hanging by the front door is a portrait of Diana and her husband. "After nearly 40 years, I think it's going to work," she said with a smile.

Tenanche
Vibrational Healer/Shaman/Reiki Master

The more I sit across from people in readings, the more I sit in circle ceremonies with women and men, the more I do healing or essence work, the more I'm healing within me. We're all in this together.

The small upstairs apartment that Tenanche shares with her husband in Tucson, Arizona, is modestly outfitted with mostly second-hand furnishings – nothing to which she's really attached. But the two- and three-dimensional art works that color this humble space are of value to the tall, slender woman of 41. Tenanche created the art as part of her healing process.

We sat on the floor of her living room one afternoon in early fall while Tenanche projected slides of her art onto an empty wall. As she described her creations – pencil drawings, acrylic paintings, mixed-media collages and found-object sculptures – she described the journey that led her into the healing arts and to the Southwest desert from her native Pennsylvania.

"I'm more of a visual person than I am a verbal person," Tenanche explained, flashing a broad smile. Talking about her art was the vehicle for telling her story, in the same way that doing art has been a vehicle for self-discovery and transformation.

Tenanche has been painting since she was about 4 years old, and has degrees in painting and art history and another in Latin American studies.

Her art supports her emotionally, and it supports her monetarily when she occasionally teaches, illustrates books or sells her works. Her bold use of color, which she came by naturally, reflects her passion for Mexican and pre-Columbian cultures (she speaks fluent Spanish). It also echoes her African- and Native American heritage.

She said her abstract, mixed-media paintings are

energy field paintings or interpretations of how she perceives energy. Her colorfully embellished totems and bottle trees are derived from Native American and African cultures and have served as themes for her community projects and exhibits. Portraits of women and self-portraits incorporate symbols and images from native cultures that are important elements of Tenanche's life or that tell stories and illustrate rituals.

Painting is a ritual for Tenanche, just like the rituals she creates for women's circles that honor their moon cycles and embrace nature and all that is feminine. I recognized one of the slides as the cover of a book she illustrated. "Songs of Bleeding" by Spider contains ceremonies and celebrations that honor women's moon cycles, earth cycles and life cycles. They were recreated and recorded by the Caney Indian Spiritual Circle of the Taino Indian community in Pittsburgh, Pennsylvania, to which Tenanche belongs. (The Tainos were the indigenous people of the Caribbean who met Columbus. Their culture has been revived in Pittsburgh by Miguel Sague.) The book's cover features one of her self-portraits. The artist stands naked, eyes fixed forward; her long, black hair covers her brown shoulders. Branches emerge from a spiral over her womb – the center of creativity – and twist upwards towards the sun above her right shoulder and the moon above her left shoulder. A snake weaves upwards through the branches, hugging her left thigh.

The original painting is 5 feet tall and was completed in 1990 following a crisis. Its title:

"Reawakening, Remembering, I Am the Life Tree: Te-nan-che." "This came after a depression and a spiritual emergence," Tenanche said. "I got sick; everything caught up with me. My immune system, my chakras, everything just shut down." To regain her health, she did visualizations, said affirmations, practiced yoga "just so I could get from the bed to the shower," got counseling and joined a recovery group. She also began dreaming and getting information about healing with crystals – an important element of the healing work she does today. "I started using the crystals on my chakras; I got information about using and drinking crystal water. That's how I got into crystal essences. I didn't know anything about it, it just came. All those things helped me to come back. Then this painting came up, and I felt that I really chose whether I was going to stay or leave." She remembered the meaning of the name she adopted while in college; she remembered she was the "Tree of Life."

Tenanche frequently receives information in her dreams, and messages often are conveyed through deceased family members. She never met her grandmother, who had the gift of healing and died when Tenanche's mother was a girl. "But I know my grandmother," Tenanche said. "She was one of the people who brought me information when I was in that depression." Her grandmother told her how to use crystals; other dreams guided her to fashion a gift for her grandmother to honor her wisdom. Tenanche honored her grandmother in her dreams; then she honored her with a sculpture – an offering – that she exhibited in a group show. "The process is like giving back to the earth, giving back to our ancestors. You make an offering, and then the healing comes."

Years ago, Tenanche's grandmother was named "Central America Moon" by a Native American visionary. So Tenanche found no coincidence in her own involvement with the Taino Indians. Tenanche connected with the Taino culture at a time when she was seeking her Native American heritage. She dressed native, adopted native ways, and was considered family as she grew proficient in Taino ceremonies through her apprenticeship with Miguel.

"When I met Miguel, the Taino shaman, in 1983, he just took me under his wing. The push started then because he saw the gifts in me and began to pull them out. He believed that I already knew this stuff. We began working together in 1984. I began doing full moon ceremonies, participating in activities at the Indian center. Then he introduced me – I'd say, reintroduced me – to shamanic journeying. Journeying is a way of going into the spirit world and finding healing there, getting in touch with spirit guides or animal spirits, bringing the healing back. Once I picked up on that, I did it a lot. I'm still doing it a bit, but have moved into other directions with my crystals and essences."

Tenanche showed me a photograph of her at age 4, dressed in a Native American outfit. She knew at that time that she wanted to be an "Indian" someday. "I feel I had a sense of what I would be doing through these healing ceremonies, through the native culture of the Tainos, as a healer, as a ceremonial leader. I've had dreams throughout my life where I dreamed I'd touch a person and they'd be healed. So I felt that someday I'd move into that. I don't touch people and then they're healed, but certainly touch is part of the healing process. People always call me a seer or tell me I'm psychic. I call myself a seer or a sensitive."

Even though she was comfortable with her place in the Taino community, Tenanche was not at peace with her African-American heritage. She experienced what she perceived as prejudice while directing ceremonies at Indian events, became depressed and stopped her involvement for a while. The long unresolved issues around her African heritage led to another painting, "Black with Indian Blood: Shame/Healing, After All, This Is America."

"It's something I had to do," she recalled. "I do the best work when I'm having a hard time emotionally; art has a healing effect. The self-portraits help me to find my identity, take all of the elements that are part of me – the African, the Taino Indian spirituality, my own Native American heritage, womanhood. Part of my struggle is having this ethnic and racial mixture; part of my journey has been to accept my African heritage. I really let the resentment get to me for while, but I'm working on healing that now. Resentment is a poison that you take yourself in order to hurt someone else. It only hurts you." Tenanche kept the painting for three years and then, like she does with many of her art works, she destroyed it. "It was time to move on."

And she has moved on. Today Tenanche appears to be in balance with her mixed heritage. She wears her hair African style, embellishing her long dreadlocks with metallic and colored beads; a colorful textile crowns her forehead. She continues to practice Taino ceremonies, does readings, energy work (such as Reiki and balancing chakras with crystals), and follows the Mayan calendar. She makes crystal and gem essences (Crystal Radiance is her line) and is beginning to combine them with flower essences.

"The flower essences are a recent development, something I feel directed to do. I always used flower essences by other companies. I'm just now beginning to develop and combine my gem essences with my own flower essences. I do research; I collect essences to see what other companies are doing. Each one of my crystal books says something different about a stone, or has variations on its use. Since I'm getting into flower essences in a new way, I also refer to books about flowers. What I offer is based on the synthesis of that and intuition. I'm not going to say that I don't use books; they're tools. It also takes a calling, a commitment and dedication."

Tenanche also created her own reading cards, which are about half the size of tarot cards. Each of the cards' hand-colored images or glyphs have specific meanings and were derived from Taino cosmology, originating from Puerto Rican and Cuban petroglyphs. The glyphs also are found on pyramids and stone altars in Central America and Mexico. Miguel helped her refine some of the images, she said.

When she does a reading, Tenanche surrounds the cards with a crystal grid that she believes enhances the reading's meaning. "But everything I do includes crystals," she laughed. "I call them spiritual readings that really focus on emotional and spiritual issues – what's going on internally. I do a lot of reading work. And I find for some reason, in spite of the fact that many times I want some of the other healing work to be the focal point – the crystal essences, the hands-on healing – that people come for the readings. It's supportive. The ritual work and readings seem to be what attracts people the most."

Most of Tenanche's clients are women, and most of them have the same issues that she is working on or has worked through – fears of self-esteem, finances, lack of confidence, relationships. "They tend to project, as I do, on outer circumstances, where it's all an inner journey. I really do believe the healing is about empowering the person to do their own healing process. And that entails having a spiritual connection within themselves."

Tenanche's own struggle to regain her health, to build her immune system, also aids her healing work. Her beaming smile and graceful presence reflect her ongoing effort to nurture herself. "The physical is a reflection of something deeper that's out of balance. My health issues represent something that is out of balance emotionally, that comes from all that dysfunctional stuff

I'm working through, which ties into certain imbalances that are spiritual. I may do rituals and have a sense of spirituality, but it's not perfect, and I'm working on that. The more I sit across from people in readings, the more I sit in circle ceremonies with women and men, the more I do essence work, the more I'm healing within me. We're all in this together. It takes a lot of courage to get better."

Surrounded by her artwork, Tenanche has many reminders of her healing journey, its ups and downs and sometimes joyful outcomes. Her courage enables her to honor who she is and share her wisdom with others. Courage also helps her to live simply and in the moment, something that's not always easy to do. The belief systems that she and her husband embrace appear to support them, as they prepare to move into the new millennium – and new age – unencumbered by old behavior patterns and materialistic values.

Healer update

Tenanche expanded Crystal Radiance Essences to include 150 essences of rose, gems, crystals and desert-cultivated flowers. In addition to her other healing work, she does essence consultations, classes, workshops and a research program that focuses mostly on roses. She recently moved to Pittsburgh, Pennsylvania.

Contact information

Tenanche
Gifts of the Life Tree
137 Kilmer Street
Pittsburgh, PA 15221
(412) 244-7788
email: rose@crystalradiance.com
website: www.crystalradiance.com

Liliana Gambarte
Spiritual Healer/Massage Therapist

My specialty is reading
for people and seeing what kind
of ceremonies they need to do
for themselves, or what kind
of cleansing they need to do.

...My specialty is getting people
back to the elements, to know
that Mother Earth is there.

Liliana Gambarte's family knew she was destined to be a healer when she cried in her mother's womb. Her grandmother, who became her primary teacher of Earth medicine, also knew that Liliana would someday leave their home in La Paz, Bolivia, and move far away to share the healing traditions of their ancestors.

That faraway place was Tucson, Arizona, where Liliana moved by chance 20 years ago. As Liliana told her life's story in the comfort of her Tucson home, her beaming face and buoyant spirit concealed her years of hardship and oppression. Tears welled in her eyes on several occasions as she talked about her family in La Paz and the great sadness that came with leaving them and her community of teachers at 16.

Liliana's grandmother told her many times throughout her childhood that she would leave Bolivia. But it was Liliana's sisters, brothers and cousins who dreamed of leaving their impoverished lives behind to have a better life in the United States, not Liliana. One of her cousins had married an American man and moved to the U.S. When the cousin briefly returned to Bolivia to take a family member back to America, the family met for seven days to decide who would go with her. When it was announced that Liliana was to go, everyone was silent.

"We come from very humble, poor people. They let you go so you can have a better life than they had," recalled Liliana, her fluent English revealing her Spanish roots. "They knew it was my calling. They chose me because they felt I had the teachings and believed that

I was a warrior, that I could defend myself no matter where I would go. I was told that I was stronger than any male in my family – emotionally, physically, spiritually; that I could take anything and not give up."

That strength and perseverance served Liliana well in the years that followed. Soon after she moved with her cousin to Columbia, Missouri, her cousin's husband asked her to move out. Liliana was on her own in a land where she did not speak the language and had only a fifth-grade education. She washed dishes to support herself and her subsequent move to the Northeast. In New York, she worked in a factory before returning to Missouri, where she began learning some English from African-American co-workers. Each time she moved, her grandmother's letters would repeat the same concern: "You need to get out of that place or your spirit will die."

Liliana worked hard and saved money to send to her sisters and to support her next move. And each time she moved she traveled in fear. "I did not have papers for a long time and was always running from Immigration people. Thankfully, Immigration was not as hard as it is now. If the bus stopped, I would pray hard. My teachers always told me that if I prayed hard enough I would become invisible, and I experienced that. The Immigration people would come into the bus, look at me and pass by and leave. In all my travels, my spirits were very kind to me."

Liliana also hid her healing gifts, fearing that people would confuse her Earth medicine with witchcraft. But that changed after a friend convinced her to move to Arizona. "For a long time I wouldn't have an altar, or I would have a small altar," Liliana said. "It wasn't until I moved to Tucson that I became more free. The spirits of Arizona were glad to see me, I think. Life has been wonderful since."

Today Liliana's altars are an extension of who she is and how she works. When I arrived at her home in late September for a reading, Liliana walked me over to her altars and recited a prayer. It was a beautiful sight. The two, knee-high altars spanned nearly the full length of a wall in her living room. They were covered with cloth and crowded with flickering candles, vases of flowers, bowls of ripening fruit and many sacred objects: shells, feathers, stones, religious figurines and pictures. And sage. Sage that she burned as we faced the altars, cleansing my aura with its healing aromatic smoke.

Liliana led me into the room where she does hour-long readings and different types of healings. We sat on the floor facing each other; she saged the space between us. She did one reading using a Mayan tarot deck and a second reading using orange and black bean-like seeds. Liliana gave me insights on different aspects of life; she gave me rituals to do for cleansing my aura and my womb, a ritual to honor the spirit of my deceased father. Information and homework, ways to reconnect with self and Earth.

"My specialty is reading for people and seeing what kind of ceremonies they need to do for themselves, or what kind of cleansing they need to do,"

Liliana later said.

"Many people come to me and say they need this healing and want me to do it. I say that you need to do this, you need to be responsible for yourself. There are some ceremonies that I have to do for them because they are very powerful, and it also depends on what problems the person has. If they have a very bad witchcraft on them, I can give them things that they can do on their own to help my work. But I have to do the last step in order to take it all out.

"My specialty is getting people back to the elements, to know that Mother Earth is there. My teachers and grandmother always told me when my mother died that your physical mother can die and your physical mother can abandon you, but there is only one true mother that we all have and that's the Earth Mother. We call her Pacha Mama. She is our true mother."

Liliana's Earth medicine is derived from her mother's Incan and Spanish roots. The rituals she learned from her grandmother and other teachers are a blend of practices used by Native Americans, Spanish gypsies and the Catholic religion. Like other healers of her tradition, she had to pass tests or initiations to earn her powers, the respect of her community and the elements – earth, air, water and fire. Part of each initiation is spent in isolation so the initiate can meditate and bring information back to the community. Each initiation and meeting with her teachers reaffirms Liliana's spiritual name, "Condor Woman/Warrior Woman." Her last initiation was in Bolivia in 1991.

"That is the role of the shaman. We get visions not just for ourselves, but for other people, for the community. That's why they put us through such hard initiations. After fasting and having to dance and dance, you have visions. Some shamans come with songs, beautiful music. I have visions of how I can help others or help myself. I can see rituals, ceremonies for others; I see how to get in touch with the stone people, the shells, the trees, and hear how they can be used for curing. That's my calling – getting in touch with the energy of nature.

"In the readings, I go back to what the elements told me and see how that would pertain to that person. I throw the seeds to see what this person needs to do. They may have to hug trees for seven days straight. It's a way for us as healers to educate them that trees also have life, trees have energy – healing energies that God gave us – and wisdom to teach us. Some people have to lie on big stones, the grace of our Mother."

Spiritual baths are a ritual Liliana frequently prescribes for clients. It's a way that they can take responsibility for their healing and to practice their faith. It's also very magical and feels great. Part of my homework was to take three baths when I returned home following a recipe of white flowers, milk and several other sweet-smelling ingredients. "Different baths call for different things," Liliana said. "I have to do what comes to me in readings. You needed to cleanse your aura so any negative energy that you had gotten along

174

the way would be washed away in the bath. What came to me was the color white, so you needed a milk bath with white flowers. Sometimes it calls for red roses."

Liliana learned how to do readings from her grandmother. The teachings began when she was 5 and living with her grandmother after her mother drowned. (She and her siblings never were close to their Italian father and his family.) Her grandmother also taught her how to do healings. When Liliana was 11, her grandmother took her to a community in the Andes, where she stayed with medicine people for nine months. At 13, she was sent to Santa Cruz in Bolivia's tropics for a year to learn tropical medicine. "I saw beautiful medicine there and learned snake wisdom," she said.

"I saw very beautiful snakes in the jungle and learned how to gather different energies from them. My job was to look at them and ask them to give me the wisdom and energy I needed for my work. Snakes go deep inside the earth and bring you wisdom from the womb of Mother Earth. They give you the energy of being a warrior, to walk your path without being afraid and to be able to speak venom only when you need to. It's both feminine and male energy.

"The reason why they sent me there is they knew I would have my first moon, and I needed to be in a tropical place to learn to walk like the palm trees. To be feminine and have the power of the palm trees, graceful and sensuous. I got the experience there I wish every woman would have: The experience of coming from a child into a woman – transformation."

Liliana remains a graceful and sensuous woman, although American culture doesn't allow the freedom of expression she enjoyed in Bolivia. (Her family tells her she walks like a stick when she returns for visits.) But her light complexion has allowed an acceptance her darker-skinned siblings would not have found here. "My family believed I was born like I was for a reason, that I would be more accepted being lighter skinned than if I would be dark colored. They said it would be easier to take my teachings wherever I go, that I would be accepted."

In Tucson, she has been accepted and supported. With friends' help, she earned her G.E.D. and a two-year degree in social services. It took her seven years to complete her undergraduate degree at the University of Arizona, and more recently, with the encouragement of her teachers in Bolivia, she graduated from the Desert Institute of Healing Arts with a certificate in massage therapy. She also studied Hawaiian massage, which she discovered was similar to Bolivian massage.

"That's why I like the Hawaiian technique, because it is very familiar. It uses a particular motion on the arms and legs, joint stretches and breathing to get movement. At home we believe that if the fluids are not going through your body, then you're not balanced."

Liliana also uses stones, shells and sticks to massage the muscles and provide clients with the earth energy they need.

"We really don't call it massage. We call it healings – a form of medicine. It comes from many generations of my people. A lot of Americans don't really care for that; they just want a plain Swedish massage. But some people are more open."

When she gave me a massage, Liliana rubbed my muscles with warm stones nestled in the palm of her hand. She also placed larger stones on my sacrum and along my spine so my body could soak up the heat. It felt wonderful. Liliana explained that stones are used to ground a person, which I needed since I had been driving for two days prior to seeing her. They also are good for depression. And Liliana sensed that I needed heat. But some people have too much fire in them and need to be cooled, so she may take them to the river and work with cold water and stones. Shells provide water energy, while sticks offer tree energy.

"We can put the stones in the fire, in the sun, in cold water, in the river and lake, depending on what the needs of the person are. The cold may be something they need to wake everything up on the cellular level so they can feel the healing power. You also have to call their spirits to come to you, call the spirits of the water, the spirits of the wind if you are doing it outside."

Whether Liliana is doing a healing or prescribing a ritual, she works from her heart and soul. She speaks from her humble roots. "I have to do what the spirits say. I would be too arrogant to say what to do. I have to ask permission from their own guide spirits. I just use what's channeled through. I cannot teach everything my teachers taught me because some ceremonies are very sacred and some ceremonies can only be done by me or higher medicine people. So I can share enough to help people to believe in themselves again and to believe that even a stone, no matter how small, can bring you some sort of healing if you have the faith."

One of Liliana's spirit guides serves to heal couples' relationships and bring fertility to women, and she often works with couples. She teaches couples how to do rituals that encourage spiritual growth, peace and love. She also offers ceremonies for women's circles. Her vision is to travel around the country and do readings, share rituals and teach the power of prayer. Her strength and determination will continue to carry her along her path, for she knows the wisdom of the snake and the miracle of prayer.

"I want to share what my teachers taught me so people can become more powerful. To teach them how to have peace. And how to be in touch with Mother Earth, the sky, all the elements of the universe so they can know they have the right to be here. We all belong here on Earth. That's my mission."

Healer update

In addition to her private practice, Liliana Gambarte has been doing group work where she introduces and teaches spirituality through ceremonies.

Contact information

Liliana Gambarte
Condor Woman/Warrior Woman
LaPaz
4050 E. Paseo Grande
Tucson, AZ 85711
(520) 881-2857

PART FIVE

CLAIRVOYANT HEALERS

Nancy Blackmore
New Age Counselor

*L*ife is really about gifts and
lessons, and that truth and love
is all there is. If we can come to
that realization, then we'll find
ourselves and be able to do what
we're here to do.

Nancy Blackmore. Her name frequently surfaced during my novice year as a massage therapist. Two clients raved about her. Hearsay from psychic fairs alluded to her popularity. So when my husband and I started talking about divorce, I knew it was time to meet this highly praised woman. "I need direction in my relationship and career," I said coyly when I called for an appointment, trying to disguise my fragility. A few months later, after Nancy and I had deepened our professional and personal relationships, the Pueblo, Colorado, psychic confided that she had intuited my marriage's demise moments after my first phone call.

In the years of monthly sessions that have followed my first reading, Nancy has guided my healing process using her gifts as a clairvoyant and telepathic, her expertise in counseling, and her gentle way of speaking and evoking the truth. It's a process she knows intimately, because in the 22 years that she has worked in the mental health field, Nancy has dedicated as much time to healing herself as she has to healing others. "I certainly had to confront my own self-denial system in order to be willing to heal myself and to offer that gift to others," Nancy said. "I'm always healing myself. It's part of the human process."

The only magic Nancy knew about as a young woman was marriage. So before she had a chance to discover the magic within herself, she got married and left the small Indiana farm community where she grew up. It was several years before she realized that she was different, that other people didn't share her ability to read minds and predict the future. She attributes most of her psychic tendencies to being a Pisces and to particular aspects in her astrological chart. "I knew things that were going to happen, even in first grade. I just went along with the usual and grew up in a dysfunctional family. Even when a lot of people were around, I was alone, fantasized a lot. As a child I was very spiritually based, was 'one' with things. I really didn't focus on what to do with it until my 20s."

It was then, in the mid-1960s as a single mother, that Nancy's psychic abilities began to resurface and she started to grow spiritually. She had no support system, so she read what limited and often outdated materials were available on metaphysical topics. (Metaphysics wasn't the household word it is today, so Nancy didn't have access to the vocabulary that was reshaping her life. "I didn't even know that what I was doing was called metaphysics," she said.) When her consciousness began to shift, she experienced one of the few "frightening" moments in her transformation. "It felt like a death – in essence a death – as if I was going to leave. It felt like there was a shroud over my head, like I was suffocating. It lasted for a couple of days, then I realized that I was shifting to another level of consciousness."

Nancy's second marriage brought her to Pueblo, where she continued to give readings (the market had greatly expanded by then) and went to college to become licensed as a mental health worker. During the 18 years she worked at an adolescent group home, she expanded her skills as a healer and spiritual teacher. She

185

studied with a numerologist and a clairvoyant, began to nurture her body through massage therapy ("I needed to learn how to be in my body"), and learned tarot, palmistry and graphology (the study of handwriting). She added past life regressions to her box of therapeutic tools "because information from the past can help change behavior and thought patterns," along with guided imagery, visualizations, a variation of Emotional Stress Release and inner child therapies.

"What different tools do is to activate different aspects of the unknown – personalities, energy, events of the day, time frames," Nancy explained. For example, she always begins her private readings by figuring one's numerology (the number of the month and year a person is in can help them understand behavioral influences) and by doing a tarot card spread. "I use colors to heal the aura and work very strongly with that in my personal life. I balance a person's energy unconsciously as I'm doing their reading. A lot of my psychic energy comes in from the right and down through my heart chakra. I feel it first, as a sensation, a vibration. I see pictures, thoughts, colors sometimes; lots of feelings, but I don't go into a trance. I can bring it on, as I will it. I've never believed in limitations and work with the 'other side' as much as I work with this side."

The other side to which Nancy refers is the realm of spirits, which can manifest itself in many ways – both positive and negative. She always welcomes this type of work – "the unusual," she calls it – and has removed displaced spirits from numerous houses.

Nancy uses her psychic and spiritual gifts in her job with the Colorado Mental Health Institute's adult substance abuse program, where she is considered one of the top counselors in her field. "I feel gifted there, blessed. There is magic in the work I do there." And she continues to work with children at a local hospital's psychiatric unit. Outside her jobs, Nancy weaves more magic through private readings, fairs and private parties. She encourages regular clients to do homework, which might include journaling, practicing visualizations, reading self-help books and anything holistic that enhances the healing process. If clients don't want to work – just want a "fix" – they usually don't return, she said.

(There were many times that I wanted Nancy to tell me that my life was going to be magically OK, that I didn't have to take responsibility for my self-destructive behavior patterns. But it would have been irresponsible and unprofessional of her to let me believe that she could fix anything. So in her gentle, honest way she helped me to be honest, even if I struggled or fell before I got it.)

"My goal with my work is to lead people back into themselves, to help them to integrate their parts, their different components, such as the adult child, male-female aspects, the spiritual and emotional bodies. As a psychic, I've learned that nothing is 'just so.' We have an option for free will. So you really only have to focus on yourself. It sounds like a selfish concept, but if you focus on your own balance, you create the harmony and balance you need to practice health. It takes practice and we're practicing life whether we subscribe to it or not. It's about being conscious of what you're practicing."

At 54, Nancy reflects, "It's been a long, long, long journey. Life is metaphysical. Our own society – because of power, control and illusion – has gotten away from truth. It's real simple: Practice truth and love and surrender to the process. Conflict is not about the process but the surrender." By practicing the process of surrender, trust and self-love, Nancy's life "has grown richer in all aspects" and supports her "abundantly." Somewhere among all of the hours she works, Nancy creates quality time to be with her companion of eight years, her two children (they're both twenty-something) and three grandchildren.

"The biggest thing I learned was that you have many choices and when you don't control it, it takes you where you need to go," Nancy said. "It's a practice of being in a state of grace, tempering your ego and being willing to trust that process. My philosophy in life is really about gifts and lessons, and truth and love is all there is. If we can come to that realization, then we'll find ourselves and be able to do what we're here to do. My journey has always been very exciting. I always say I'm just getting started. I've been saying that for 15 years and will be saying that the rest of my life."

Contact information

Nancy Blackmore
88 Princeton St.
Pueblo, CO 81005
(719) 561-4165

Nan Blake
Clairvoyant Healer/Teacher

I can't heal anyone, but people can heal themselves. What I can do is teach people ways to become more aware of who they are and what's going on in their bodies.

Nan Blake climbed a mountain for the first time at age 50. It was during the Harmonic Convergence in August 1987, when people around the world joined hands, hearts and minds to initiate Earth's healing journey. It was an event that changed many lives, including Nan's. She recalled her experience as "very magical," and from the magic came the strength and courage to face the challenges that followed her climb.

Nan told her story at a friend's house in Pueblo, Colorado, where she was visiting before returning to Santa Fe, New Mexico. Nan has lived out of suitcases and boxes for some time now, traveling between Southern Colorado, Northern New Mexico and Sedona, Arizonia, where she teaches at the School of Energy Mastery and "heals healers." For the past eight months, she has taught and traveled in Europe and Egypt. Her giant Schnauzer didn't leave her side as we talked, determined not to be left behind again.

The same year Nan climbed Greenhorn Mountain, which lies to the south of Pueblo, her 25-year-old son, Mitchell, was diagnosed with cancer. Nan was a weaver at the time, and she and her husband raised llamas on a farm in Gardner, Colorado. Mitchell decided to pursue alternative health care in addition to the medical treatments he was receiving. "My family had meditated and been on a spiritual quest for a long time," Nan said. "The whole family got involved and started looking for information on how to treat cancer alternatively. That's how I got involved in healing – checking out books, just searching and finding out what would work."

The search led them to Dr. Bernie Seigel's book, "Love, Medicine and Miracles," and then to Denver where they attended one of Seigel's workshops. "On the last day of the workshop it was announced that Barbara Ann Brennan was doing a workshop the following week," Nan recalled. "I had just started to read her first book, 'Hands of Light,' two days before we went to Denver. To make a long story short, I attended Brennan's workshop and signed up for her school."

So in the midst of her son's illness, Nan began a four-year commitment to Brennan's school. It required trips to New York City for six four-day intensives each year and private sessions with a healer between classes. During her second year of school, Nan began to explore other avenues in the alternative healing field. She was en route to Los Angeles to attend a workshop by a noted psychic healer when she was sidetracked by a workshop by Dr. Robert Jaffe at his School of Energy Mastery in Sedona. She enrolled in Jaffe's school after his workshop and spent the next three years attending two schools.

Nan's brown eyes sparkled and her Boston accent punctuated her speech as she recalled those years of exhilaration and pain. "I didn't go to school to heal Mitchell. I got interested in what was going on in the healing field. Years ago I had the feeling that I would do something with my hands some day. I used to feel energy running out of my hands when I would meditate, but I didn't know what it meant. Then in 1982, a psychic worked with a meditation group I was in and told each of us something about our future. She gave me a one-liner; 'You will be a healer of healers.' I didn't know what it meant and was terribly disappointed because all the other people were told these really interesting things. But I understand it now."

Mitchell died three years after he was diagnosed with cancer. During that time, there were great healings in their family, Nan said. "It was extremely painful and it's something I wouldn't want to go through again. I didn't have the vision then that I have now, but I watched him as he connected with different realities before he died. He was going through the process of being interdimensional, working on his own past lives; there was information coming in for him and three guides working with him. Some people might have said he was crazy and hallucinating, but I was living in the hospital with him and the stories had continuity. We didn't jar him from the level he was on. That's what he did the last six weeks before he died. It was amazing.

"So I continued on. By that time I was quite involved in school, and it was a place where I could heal myself and the great pain of losing a child. I was opening my own awareness to other worlds and realities, looking at death in a way I never looked at before. In school, I also had support to deal with the physical aspects of my grief, which were real, profound and very painful."

Nan faced and healed her grief, but her husband turned his grief inward and became ill. He died two years after Mitchell's death. "He couldn't bear to watch Mitchell die, so he pulled away and then kept it all bottled up," Nan said. "I was instrumental in helping my husband make the transition into spirit, because by that time I could see what was happening. I was with him when he left his body and actually saw and assisted the spirit guides as he left. So I got to believe in this work firsthand."

Today Nan uses her vision and heightened awareness when she teaches and guides healings. This is something she never would have imagined doing as a child. Nan had many clairvoyant and out-of-body experiences until she was about 10, then consciously turned off her sight. Her sight wasn't functional, she said, and made her angry because what she saw in her experiences didn't correspond to reality. Now she knows how to balance the two worlds.

As a teacher, Nan helps students develop their awareness of energy in themselves and others. "I don't think there's ever a time we don't feel energy. We are energetic beings – energy is always there. I think we read energy all the time, see it all the time. I can't pick a moment when I became conscious of this. It keeps opening like a flower – there's just more and more. I don't think there's an end, just more and more consciousness."

She prefers to work with small groups of students and assists individuals in their own healing process outside the classroom. "I can't heal anyone, but people can heal themselves. What I can do is teach people ways to become more aware of who they are and what's going on in their bodies. The energy I bring in is helpful.

That's one of the things I do at school: Hold the energy for the entire student body. Part of our job is to pay attention to where students are in their classwork and who needs help. Also just to watch the energy in the room, to keep the energy high. I do this by centering myself and expanding my awareness of consciousness. I can form a container, go under the energy of the group and lift it. Or I can be the anchor and hold the energy in place."

When she does healing work, Nan combines techniques she learned at both schools with information she receives from her spirit guides. "My intention is just to be in the moment with the person I'm working with and see what comes up," she said. She laughed as she referred back to the psychic's prediction of healing healers. "Right now it's most exciting for me to work with somebody who already has a certain level of consciousness, because then we can go deeper into the work. I think I have more to contribute at that point, and they're much more willing to dive into these newer realms of healing."

Nan admits there aren't many guide books available for this type of work, especially the realm of energy work called psychic surgery. "It's something you can't teach from a book. It's usually done with a high level of guidance coming through, and at this point in time I don't think we have a whole lot of scientific background on this. In time we will. Psychic surgery is really helpful for people who have had physical surgery, because their energy fields get ripped and torn and they need to be put back together again. There are many different levels of surgery on the etheric field."

How does she do this? "Awareness activates energy. So I begin by putting my attention on a block in the client's energy field. The client then brings their attention to it and describes what they feel. A block is just condensed light. It's as if you took this . . ." Nan paused, picked up a piece of tissue and crinkled it into her hand. "Now it's not so light anymore. What happens is that if you bring attention to it – and attention is energy – it begins to move.

"The idea is to unfold it and heal it. That's basically what you're doing when you work with the etheric field. Darkness, which is the energy block, is really nothing but the absence of light or light that has been condensed. So when you bring in light, you bring a higher vibration into a lower, denser vibration. That's the principle of energetic therapies; it creates movement and things unfold. It's all flow. It's not about me going in and pulling something out. If I did that, it would come back; the hole would attract energy of a lower vibration again. The healing takes place through the client's awareness and through learning why the block is there and the lessons that come with it.

"We don't work just on the etheric field. We work on different levels – mental, emotional, spiritual, physical and etheric. When we take the healing to the higher soul level, then the block is gone forever. If we can remove the congestion from the etheric field, then it won't seed in the body. This is the easiest place to heal.

It's preventative medicine.

"As long as we're in the human body, getting healthy is constant work. No one can fix us. There are going to be problems, and there are all of the things we'd like to ditch, especially the aspects that are horny toads and slippery and slimy. It's about owning those things we don't want anybody to see. Love is the core. You can only go so far if you don't love yourself."

Nan does other types of healing work, and there hasn't been much written about them either. She calls one of them simply land work, which involves clearing blocks from land masses. She feels that her purpose is to heal the Earth as well as its people. "My experience," Nan explained, "is that I go into the land. I actually take the form of land and water – see it, feel it. I'm out of my body, but on some level I know I'm still in my body. I clear out dark areas, open channels and put in light. There's always other beings there working with me."

She also creates energy vortexes or light portals to provide passage for beings from one dimension to another. "There are a lot of beings in the astral plane that need to move on. They can be helped by light portals in the earth, a place where they could energetically move into the light and clear themselves. Sometimes you see the beings, sometimes you see light. I don't totally understand it, but I've watched it work. You can put portals anywhere."

Although she doesn't understand some of the work she does or where it is taking her, Nan remains excited about her journey and feels that it's the

198

beginning of greater things to come. It appears that she continues to manifest the magic she experienced seven years ago when she climbed her first mountain.

"This is the freest I've ever been in my life. I'm totally committed to the work I'm doing and am watching it unfold. The biggest thing has been my willingness to step into the dark abyss of unknowingness and to know that I'm going to be supported. My children say that I've finally reached my teenage years. I married and had children when I was very young, have always been responsible and involved with family. All of a sudden I'm finding that I'm flying, picking up threads I've dropped at times in my life.

"Most of all I'm enjoying the spiritual connection. This work is about being able to bring this kind of energetic level into everyday life. If I can't do it for myself, I certainly can't teach it."

Healer update

Nan Blake co-taught a group of experienced healers, teachers, business people and mystics with Barbara Kittredge in 1998 and 1999. They explored energy, expanded consciousness and the practical application of spirituality in daily life. Nan works with a similar group in Santa Fe.

She also teaches healing and consciousness-raising techniques, encourages and assists others to create spiritual support groups, and has a private telephone practice as a spiritual counselor.

Contact information

Nan Blake
2212 Copita Lane
Santa Fe, NM 87505
(505) 988-5006
email: nan@kopavi.com

Billie Cash Miller
Psychic

It's very easy for people to look to a psychic as a god. I can help them with the spirit world and the things that are going on around them that they cannot see. But they have to make their own decisions.

P sychic Billie Cash Miller is anything but pretentious. She gives readings in her modest Albuquerque home, where we visit on this first evening of January, surrounded by books, plants and memorabilia. We sit directly across from each other in the same way she works with clients during readings. Billie's style is gentle and direct; her language simple yet expressive with just a hint of her Texas roots. Her eyes twinkle as she speaks softly about her seven decades on Earth – her losses and her miracles – repeating several times that life is "just wonderful."

This is no ordinary 72-year-old. Billie does readings and healing work in her spare time – after she works a minimum of 40 hours a week in the records department at Lovelace Medical Center; after she walks 3 miles each morning and works out at a gym for an hour after work. "I thoroughly enjoy what I do," Billie said. "One of these days I'm going to retire and do readings full time – if I ever get to that point. I'm in excellent health. I take vitamins, take care of myself. You can't take anything for granted, especially when you get as ancient as I am."

Although Billie's appearance is grandmotherly, her energy belies her age. Her responses to my questions are simple but articulate. Her presence is warm and gentle; her elfin nature shows on her face and in the sparkling polish she wears on her fingernails.

Billie began doing readings about 25 years ago after developing her psychic and healing abilities through classes on unfolding at Albuquerque's Holy Spirit

Church. She hasn't always been psychic and doesn't recall any psychics in her family. It all started about 30 years ago when she was working as a secretary and medical assistant for a psychiatrist. "I was seeing visions on the wall, and I thought, boy, that's all I need," she recalled. "Things just started happening all at once. It frightened me at first, especially when I couldn't turn it off. It was like looking at a moving picture. I thought, 'My word, he's going to have me committed if I don't watch what I'm doing here.' It finally subsided."

That was when Billie sought a teacher, whom she found at the spiritualist church. The unfolding classes taught "a little of everything," including hands-on healing using colors and other forms of visualization. One of her first experiences with group healing involved a woman with a brain tumor. By collectively visualizing the woman's tumor, the group was able to shrink the tumor, Billie said. "This was a joint effort – there were some very strong healers in that church. The doctors were startled. They expected to do surgery and didn't have to."

The psychiatrist for whom Billie worked also served as a catalyst for her psychic growth. "He was a fantastic man and a close friend," Billie said. "At first, things would come up and he would say, 'How did you know that?' And I'd say, 'I'm psychic.' He enjoyed testing me to see if I knew what I was talking about. I always did, and many times it was of great benefit to him."

Billie's gifts are equally respected at the hospital

where she has worked for the past 23 years. "I'm the first dream interpreter in the medical records department," Billie laughed. She enjoys interpreting dreams for the department's 'youngsters.' "I'm very fond of young people anyway. If they have something they don't understand, I'm the first one they grab."

When friends are in the hospital, Billie does healings on them with her son, Charlie, who also works at Lovelace and shares his mother's psychic abilities. "We only work on people we know. I wouldn't think of healing someone who wouldn't ask for it. We start before surgery and end when they leave. That's very helpful because it keeps the patients from getting nauseous from the surgery and anesthesia. I was hoping that our hospital would go to touch healing, and I'm really disappointed that we didn't. But if someone comes in that we know, we still heal them. And I think that's wonderful."

Billie and Charlie heal as a team most of the time and do healing sessions in the home they share. "A person sits in the chair: One of us is in front and one of us is behind, and we're both laying our hands on and seeing the same thing. Usually when we're healing someone with kidney problems, they vibrate when we lay on the hands because of the double energy. We heal everything, but kidneys are what we do best. I have no idea why, I think people have a lot of specialties in healing, and that just happened to be ours."

During a healing session, Billie explained, "We get a picture in our head, usually. We had a trance medium for many years and were told during trance that the strongest color was the color of love. The color of love is a soft red. So when I'm healing someone, I picture a red cloud the color of love completely, totally surrounding them. I mentally tell them how I'm healing them and that they're going to completely pull this color into their physical body and start getting better. And that's what happens. They come back, and we do it again. Or I do distance healings, where you can heal someone from a distance, and I use the same effort there. They are not aware that they are absorbing the color, but they are doing it. There are so many things like that that have happened."

Billie's ministerial work at Holy Spirit Church has fostered many healing and reading opportunities throughout the years. Now she does healings and readings for people from all over the country and works with them in person, over the phone and through the mail. There was a time when Billie did readings for Psychic Friends, a national psychic telephone service that was the "darndest thing I ever saw." She may resume working with the psychic line after she retires.

"Usually people come for readings because they're in trouble, they're upset or they're depressed and they need answers. They need to feel that they're not alone. They come back every six weeks or so for additional readings or until things are working well for them. And when I don't see them anymore, then I know that they're really on their own. So I feel very good about it. People don't depend on me because I tell them that I don't want them to take my word verbatim for anything, that I want them to seek and find their own answers. It's very easy for people to look to a psychic, especially a good psychic, as a god, to ask what this or that they should do or buy. I can help them with the spirit world and the things that are going on around them that they cannot see. But they have to make their own decisions."

Giving readings is like being on a radio wave, Billie said. "I can tell – I click – when I have touched into your vibration. I usually take a deep breath and let it out slowly, and then I feel everything that you feel on all levels. I can feel your pain, but I can feel all your happiness, too. It's hard to explain what I do. But my teachers – spirit teachers – give me messages to give to my clients. Whenever I give a reading, I always ask for their teachers to be present. Usually we have a houseful around here, and all during the readings you can hear the walls pop, the TV pops – like a communication going on. The client hears it, too.

"The pops are just energy. My teachers have a system. One knock is yes – it's like a confirmation. Two knocks are no; three is a change in condition that's coming in. I explain to clients what it means, and they start listening for all they're worth. I tell them to pay attention to raps when they're home and what it means; to remember what they're thinking, because Spirit will confirm something they thought. They really have to be on the ball to interpret it correctly."

Billie doesn't use many metaphysical tools, such

as tarot cards. ("I wasn't accurate at all with them," she said.) She mostly works with what she sees and hears, "cleans" auras, pulls in past life information when needed, sends angels to help people. But she occasionally uses power probes, which answer questions much like a pendulum does and are useful for skeptical clients. The power probes are two metal wires shaped like an "L" that the users hold loosely in their hands. The longer ends are held parallel to each other and the floor and move together when the answer to a question is yes, or move apart when the answer is no. The probes point to lost objects as well. Billie also uses a crystal ball, mostly for meditation. "I get visions in the crystal ball – like the visions I saw on the wall, but I know the meaning of them. I can ask questions, and they come through."

Billie heals herself on occasion in the same manner she heals others and usually is assisted by her son. In 1988, she was hospitalized with congestive heart failure, asthma and diabetes. When she got out of the hospital, Charlie told her that he signed her up for a walking race. (Charlie runs marathons.) "And I said, you signed me up for what?" Billie recalled. "I could hardly walk, was pulling oxygen, which I pulled for a year and a half. So I started walking in the walk races, went back to work pulling oxygen, and I had some phenomenal experiences. It was like a miracle, a small one, but a miracle." Billie attributes her recovery to walking, the power of thought and Charlie's hands-on healing. The only physical problems she acknowledges are the weakness in her left arm and her arthritic left hand. The symptoms resulted from too much radiation for the breast cancer she had 46 years ago.

It's clear that Billie still has work to do on Earth and isn't going to let age slow her down. "What I'm doing I consider to be a very great gift. I feel that my purpose is to help other people, and that's what I do. It doesn't matter to me whether they have money or not. If they need a reading, they need a reading – they need guidance. I'm never going to get rich being a psychic, but I sure enjoy it. I've met so many wonderful people. I feel like I've had just a wonderful life."

Healer update

Billie Cash Miller retired from her job at Lovelace Medical Center and quit her church involvement. She does in-person and phone readings at home.

Contact information

Billie Cash Miller
544 Cardenas SE
Albuquerque, NM 87108
(505) 266-1365

Dorothy Wood Espiau
Clairvoyant Healer/Teacher

*Humankind has forgotten
who they are. My Gems programs
teach people that they are the
gems, and they are worthy of
their gifts. What's been missing
is our capacity to love ourselves
on the highest level.*

Dorothy Wood Espiau greeted me at her spacious Sedona, Arizona, home wearing a T-shirt she had just received from a friend. It featured characters from the Disney movie, "The Lion King," encircled by the theme song's title, "Circle of Life." The shirt holds special meaning for Dorothy because she has used Disney stories as healing metaphors since she began working with children seven years ago in her Circles of Life program.

Dorothy introduced each of the miniature plastic Disney characters that filled a kitchen window ledge: Ariel from "The Little Mermaid," Aladdin, Snow White and the seven dwarfs. We laughed about the prince who was unable to stand without a prop. (He's not our type, we agreed.) "Beauty and the Beast" and the innocent Simba and regal Mufasa from "The Lion King" are among her best-loved and most-used characters and teachers. "I can talk to children in 'Lion King' language, and shifts can occur because they can see through the metaphor," Dorothy said.

She works with the wounded child in adults as well. Childhood scars, like the one worn by Scar Face in "Lion King," can distort one's vision of the world and produce limiting and self-destructive behavior patterns, she said. "I know that so many of us have been broken by the scars of our childhood. Scars represent lack of nurturing. When scars aren't taken off, they continue to run the computer."

Dorothy uses the computer metaphor to illustrate how people live their lives. "What you see in your life at this moment is what you have in your computer," she explained. "All of a person's experiences, whether positive or negative, act as programs within that computer. Emotional scars continue to affect one's life – even if they were caused years ago – unless the scars are removed or the computer is reprogrammed."

Seeing her role as a computer reprogrammer, Dorothy began creating methods or programs to undo the scars and wounds carried in the human computer. "Gems of Excellence" is one of 15 programs she has written and taught worldwide since 1987. And she has created thousands of other programs based on individuals' needs, she said, addressing everything from health problems to addictions and phobias to financial and career problems.

"Basically, Gems connects you with that place within you that enables you to know all, be all, see all, do all. Four of the programs – the most important ones – put people in harmony with their own creation. All creation is derived from mathematics. So, if you have numbers or geometry missing from the computer, then you are not in full creation."

Dorothy's keen intuitive abilities enable her to read a person's field – the space surrounding the body that she describes as the multi-dimensional blueprint that determines who we are. She also refers to the field as the human computer or "Book of Records," which contains our "memory bands of God." "It's more than an energy field. I see it as a unified field – thousands of fields. It's the human electrical memory field.

"Field is really the new frontier," Dorothy

emphasized. "I see the entire geometry of creation and have been working diligently to understand it. Humans hold within them the records – details of their lives on all levels of their existence. But humankind has forgotten who they are. Certain people are coming forth at this time to set the records straight.

"What I am dedicated to, as we move into the new millennium, is the rapid transformation – the clearing – humans must undergo to overcome their lifetimes of illusion. My Gems programs teach people that they are the gems and that they are worthy of their gifts. What's been missing is our capacity to love ourselves on the highest level.

"I looked at the geometries that I was working with all those years ago with the children, with my own life, and I realized that the circle was the most complete geometry of all. It is the beginning, the end. And I saw how the integrations were creating a new life for people, that sometimes they completed a circle of life and moved into a new circle of life. The scars were gone, another person had emerged. That circle of life became a greater circle of life."

To demonstrate how Circles of Life works, Dorothy selected an integration from her Gems program that would erase my childhood scars. "An integration," she explained, "is a process that returns the brain function to its perfect operation. It begins with setting a goal. Usually the computer's old program over-rides the goal because the body does not accept the goal as truth. This is determined by muscle testing the client after he or she states the goal. Then the reprogramming begins."

The Gems program uses a series of equations (like 9-9-6-3-7) that are orally stated while the person traces geometric patterns, mostly circles, directly over the body. These equations are the language or "software solutions" that locate and correct the computer errors, Dorothy explained. Expression of feelings, gestures, actions and visualizations might be used throughout the integration, and muscle testing is repeated to check that the computer is receiving the new information. When the process is completed – it can take 30 minutes to several hours depending on the type of integration – the goal is restated and tested. "Once wounds are resolved, they are resolved forever," Dorothy said.

The type of integration determines the manner in which a person processes the new information in the weeks or months that follow. And it is a process. "You're going to go home with whatever program that you need to find yourself," Dorothy said during my integration. As she waited for the right equation to "click" in my field, she told stories that would help me understand the true source of the computer errors or scars.

My childhood scars weren't much different from the scars most people wear; not much different from Dorothy's. As I watched this big-hearted dynamo work and play in her kitchen – her favorite playground – with her dog and three cats nuzzling for attention, it was difficult to imagine the Dorothy of the past. Today, she is bright-eyed, energy-packed and self-directed. She is living proof that Circles of Life works. But nearly 30 years ago she began having health problems that led to exhausted adrenal glands, hypoglycemia, environmental sensitivities, cancer and near-death experiences.

Most of Dorothy's problems began in her native California when a dentist did unnecessary work. "From the moment he did that dental work, I was never well again," Dorothy recalled. "He caused mercury poisoning, put incompatible substances in my mouth, disrupted the entire energy flow in my mouth. His work systematically caused the lights of my life to go out and sent me into a 25-year health crisis that I could not have comprehended at the time." She hardly remembers the prescription drug-filled years that followed.

Several years later, Dorothy and her husband moved to Houston, Texas, with their infant son. That's when she began to find answers to her many questions and where she met her mentors. One woman taught Dorothy how to use the pendulum to read subtle energies and helped her to redevelop the gift of clairvoyance that she lost as a child. The second woman – an "advanced soul" – taught Dorothy how to tend to her own soul. "Through her advanced thinking, she opened up so many things for me. She kept me alive and taught me to be there for other people." These women also helped restore Dorothy's faith in herself and in God.

Dorothy began working with a noted Chinese acupuncturist to help identify the sources of his patients' dental problems. Before the Chinese doctor left Houston, the team's popularity brought three-month waiting lists. "I used to be known as the Tooth Fairy," Dorothy laughed. But although her stamina and emerging gifts seemed to propel her forward, Dorothy continued to be sick. "I was allergic to everything in the 20th century – literally was becoming more and more reactive to everything around me. So I continued to study philosophy and theology and to run my catering business. I would sit with my oxygen tank and talk to God."

She finally found a doctor at the Nevada Clinic in Las Vegas, Nevada, who put her on her feet again. Along the way, she began to see that the relationships with her husband and her church were also contributing to her ill health. And she realized that she didn't know how to nurture herself. "Most people with immune system disorders don't get well because they don't know how to nurture themselves," Dorothy said.

Another turning point in Dorothy's recovery followed her introduction to brain re-education through Paul Dennison's Educational Kinesiology or Edu-K. "Edu-K enabled me to verbalize what I knew for the first time. Then information started coming through. It wasn't a miracle, I just overcame my dyslexia." That led to the writing of her first program based on her needs and the needs of a little girl who suffered brain damage at birth.

"It was 1987, the year of the Harmonic Convergence. I wrote the first Gems of Excellence program with the assistance of pure spirit. It changed my life. As I began writing this work, I had a very strong focus on children and worked a lot with disabled children's schools. A big focus for me is that next generation. As I attempted to go out and do this, God became more paramount in my life. I'm happiest when I'm teaching in front of a group. I just consider myself as a conduit for God. I listen, and in the moment, I create."

Every time Dorothy resisted following her new path, she got sick again. So she got divorced and spent two years on the road, teaching and "finding fragments of the human race." A speaking engagement at a dental conference brought her to Sedona. "I drove into this valley and realized that I was home. It matched my hair," Dorothy laughed. (At 52, her hair matches Sedona's more pastel reds.) Although she offers two- or three-day private sessions at her Sedona home and does integrations in conjunction with her teaching and speaking engagements, she believes that teaching is her stewardship. Her newly founded Sedona School of Field Mastery is just one of many offerings of her parent company, the International Success Institute.

"I consider myself a sacred geometrist, which means that I see things in God's language. I read what the records say, see patterns of illness. I look and listen for spelling errors in the system. The human body carries the frequency of correction and all we have to do is get the body to stay in agreement with that. We don't need to heal, we just need to get the interference out of the way. My work takes chaos and nudges it into order. Then I teach people how to read the records. It's just clearing them enough to see it, to hear it."

Dorothy also calls herself an alchemist. "That's why I was so effective when I was a caterer. People wanted to know, how do you make your cakes so good? We just put love in it, energy in it. It's about working with the vibrations. Like the movie, 'Like Water for Chocolate,'" Dorothy said with a laugh. "I still work a lot in alchemy, in bringing the cells and elements of the body into balance." She created a line of scented sprays for cleansing and protection. Vanilla and rose essential oils offer protection from negative entities, she said. Her company also carries an extensive line of products for balancing the physical, mental, emotional and spiritual bodies.

Future plans include creating more programs and working with medical researchers to correct DNA distortions. She also is enjoying her age and the wisdom that comes with it, she said, and looks forward to being a grandmother someday. She has two sons.

And so the circle continues to grow. The circle – an ever-present term in Dorothy's vocabulary. On this warm spring day in Sedona, conversation with Dorothy always circles back to "The Lion King." She becomes animated as she enacts her favorite scene when the Pride Land regained its natural beauty and balance after its scar was removed. Mufasa was feeling lost, confused and hopeless when the voice of his father bellowed from the spirit kingdom: "Remember who you are." Dorothy wants humankind to do the same.

Contact information

Dorothy Wood Espiau
Circles of Life
Integrated Health Solutions
International Success Institute
P.O. Box 2788
Sedona, AZ 86339
toll free: (800) 959-3773
fax: (800) 514-0116

PART SIX

ANIMAL HEALERS

Kate Solisti
Animal Communicator

Being an animal communicator is really about being the vehicle for this information so that people can begin to understand who these beautiful beings are in our lives.

Lyris, my 6-year-old canine companion, lay facing me on the bed in our cabin at Ojo Caliente Mineral Springs in New Mexico. The warm March sun streamed through the south-facing windows as our guest, Kate Solisti, and I talked about – and with – my schnauzer-cocker spaniel. Kate is an animal communicator, a telepathic interpreter who helps dog lovers like me hear what their animal companions have to say.

"This often happens when we do this kind of work," Kate said about Lyris' sleepy appearance. "The animal completely conks out and goes into a very deep space." When I noted that Lyris was quietly tracking our conversation, Kate laughed. "She doesn't miss a thing. This is one dog that is so aware. I think even if she is in a deep, deep sleep, there's always a part of her that's present and paying attention."

During the hour we talked with Lyris, Kate provided information about the dog's purpose in my life, her behavior with certain people, a particular physical condition, her past lives, our past lives together. I asked the questions, Lyris gave the answers. "She thinks this is pretty funny, actually," Kate said after my opening question. "Lyris says, 'I think we're going to do a lot of review today for Kate's benefit.'" That was true. It was not the first time Lyris and I had worked with healers.

Kate does similar readings for people by phone or mail from her home in Santa Fe, New Mexico. Clients call or fax information from throughout the United States and Europe, something she's very excited about. Their interests range from wanting to deepen their relationships with their animals to needing assistance with training and performance, breeding and neutering, health issues and behavior counseling. "Most people who contact me are aware and open to the possibility that their animal has something to say. Animals are quite evolved and are here to facilitate their person's path and their own path, their souls' development," Kate said.

Clients may hear Kate's gentle, nurturing voice, which shows no hint of her northern New Jersey roots – "It's the voice training I did while I was in theater," she said when I told her she sounds British at times. But phone clients don't often see the blue-eyed woman who stands 6 feet tall in Western boots and loves the embellishment of earrings and scarves.

Although Kate and I talked mostly about dogs, this sweet-natured 37-year-old works with all of humankind's companion animals – especially dogs, cats and horses – and is clearly focused on healing humanity and the planet. "Our companion animals have made a conscious choice to be with us in situations very difficult for most animals. They have chosen to help us heal, to help us feel loved, so we can find our way home, back to Source (God). This is a tremendous gift, for when we truly receive the love of another, whether it's a human being or animal being, we recognize in ourselves our own innate lovability. Then we can believe that we are loved by Creator, by Source, and that we are part of Source, that we are part of a whole family. I think human beings are truly longing for this."

Kate has worked diligently to bridge the world

of humans and animals since 1993, about four years after she reopened to her psychic abilities. She tells many wonderful and miraculous stories about her dog and cat clients, but my favorite story is about a tabby cat named Dusty, who became her constant companion and first teacher when Kate was 3 years old. "From my earliest memories, I have been able to hear animals talk," Kate wrote in a story for Tiger Tribe magazine. "I was talking to trees and birds and animals before I could talk to people. In fact, I don't know if it was because of my special ability, but as a child I felt more at ease in the natural world of animals than in the world of people. And so I had been longing for a special friend who would understand me and with whom I could talk. Dusty was the answer to my prayers."

Dusty and Kate were inseparable as they played, talked and slept together. He told her that humans had forgotten how to hear animals, but that someday they would remember. He told her that her purpose in life was to help people remember their connection to animals. Although Kate preferred being with Dusty when she began school, he started to detach from her and encouraged her to be with people. She didn't know that his work with her was done. Dusty died after being hit by a car, and Kate was grief-stricken and became sick. Within two years of Dusty's death, she lost her connection to the natural world of animals and plants; she developed cat allergies when she was 12.

It wasn't until she entered therapy with her husband, David, about 10 years ago that Kate realized

230

she had shut down her feminine, intuitive side while growing up. Losing Dusty and battling with her father during adolescence caused her to operate from her masculine side. As she began to reintegrate the masculine and feminine, her psychic abilities began to return. Her dog wouldn't talk to her (he still doesn't talk much), but she began to hear the trees. "The trees wouldn't talk to me when I was stressed out and needed them. It was a powerful lesson about being. What I discovered was that when we need something, we're pushing out energy, we're not in a place to receive. But from a place of waiting, a yin place, then we can get the gifts we seek."

What Kate and her husband needed was to slow their frenzied lifestyle of commuting from Maryland to jobs in Washington, D.C., where Kate worked for a national environmental organization. So they did just that. Kate's job shift to a field office for the Nature Conservancy brought the couple to Santa Fe six years ago. And as Kate and David continued to heal themselves, Kate discovered that she no longer fit into the world of corporate thinking. So she quit her job, took a Reiki class and became a psychic's apprentice.

One of her assignments was to work on a dog that belonged to one of the psychic's clients. The dog was full of tumors and was dying because he thought he wasn't loved or special. As a puppy, he misinterpreted his human's actions as she groomed and pampered two of his litter mates before she took them to a show to be sold. He never got the message that he was the chosen one, the one she loved. So for years he internalized his lack of worth until his body was riddled with sickness. Two weeks after Kate communicated his story and his human told him how she really felt, the dog's tumors disappeared.

So began Kate's foray, as she likes to call it, into her work as an animal communicator – and healer. Because in many cases, like this dog's, the information she communicates is enough to restore health to the animal and balance to the relationship. Kate gained more experience by volunteering to do Reiki at a holistic veterinary clinic. "My work just grew from there. I continued to do Reiki, to listen and learn, to compare what the animal would communicate to what the vet records said. The more I learned, the more I was asked (by Source) to grow and continue to do my own work, to go farther into the work and bring in more of the esoteric."

Then Kate met Shelley Donnelly, another animal healer. "Shelley taught me a tremendous amount, such as how to focus better, how to clarify and refine my abilities. She has worked with psychics for a long time and is doing extraordinary work for animals from her base in France." Kate spends time with Shelley each year, and together they continue to learn more about the mental, emotional, physical and spiritual natures of our companion animals. The two are part of a movement of animal psychics and healers that has been blossoming for the past five years, Kate said.

"There have been a few individuals – writers, practitioners – doing this work for approximately

25 years. There's more of a movement now because personal healing has been heightened by the light and support coming in from the angelic realm. As we connect with ourselves, we learn that animals are eager to help us reconnect with our path to wholeness."

Animal communication is not a new concept. According to Kate, English huntmasters are so connected to their dogs by what they call a "golden thread" that they can direct their dogs with their thoughts. Equestrians use telepathy to guide their horses through routines. Farmers mentally call in their cows, while their cows communicate with them when an animal is sick in the field. Cats have an older history, Kate said. This is what one cat told her: "We were not worshiped in ancient Egypt because we were excellent mousers or because we were pretty. We had very important work to do with the priests and priestesses. We would work in the temples with the healers to augment their natural healing abilities. In other words, we became a transmitter for extra energy. The sphinx position is the preferred position for the cats to go into to achieve that pure meditative state. The sculpture of the sphinx with the human head on the cat body is the ideal blending of human intellect and feline healing talent."

Throughout history, cats have worked with healers, Kate continued. "They actually would sometimes take the healer into the woods and guide them to plants and help them communicate with the plants. Of course, this partnership worked great up until the Middle Ages. The idea of witches' familiars being cats is no accident, because the cats were always working with healers. Then all hell broke loose, and the cats told me that they actually shifted their vibrations because it became so dangerous for them and humans. So they turned down their volume, their vibration. It's only been in the last couple of years that it's begun to be turned up again."

Cats are natural healers because they maintain a constant connection to both the Earth and Source – what Kate calls a vertical connection. "They teach us that they can be completely connected and Earth-centered and at the same time have a connection and knowledge of Source. They bring and join the two in their bodies constantly. They're also extraordinary healers because of their ability to detach. When they take on negative energy they massage it, transform it, release it, and nobody even knows they're dealing with it."

Like cats, dogs can read a person's thoughts, energy fields and sometimes past lives. But dogs are less-skilled healers and often have to take on that which they are trying to heal, sometimes to their own demise. The dog's gifts to humans are loyalty and unconditional love. They maintain energetic tethers to their humans' hearts as a way of monitoring and balancing energy. "A dog sends out a beam of love to us all the time. It has the effect of balancing and holding the human in a space of unconditional love, which then allows the human being to know on a deep level that they have unconditional support and love. It helps humans to become who they truly are. That's how a dog does its particular mission."

Kate's mission, through her readings, workshops and writing, is to inform people that animals are sentient beings worthy of respect. "In fact, equal beings," she emphasized. "Being an animal communicator is really about being the vehicle for this information so that people can begin to understand who these beautiful beings are in our lives. Humans get wrapped up with humans, thinking that we have intellect and animals don't. Animals have an innate intelligence that is a blending of heart and mind, unlike the human intellect that has created so much separation. Animals have the ability to be, and we have lost that. The important thing is we have an opportunity to reconnect and to find our place in balance on the planet, not just with each other, but with the entire planet through the wisdom of the animals and the plants."

People who take Kate's workshops learn tools to quiet and focus the mind and gain an understanding of the way animals work with energy and love. "Even if they don't learn how to communicate as I do, and I have people who simply don't get it, they will always walk away from the workshop with a sense of seeing animals in another light and begin to relate to animals differently from that point on."

Kate's work also includes maintaining close ties to holistic veterinarians and other health practitioners, to whom she refers clients when necessary. All this she balances with her personal life, staying healthy and mothering her 3-year-old daughter. "I have a commitment to staying clear on a daily basis. I hope that living this way will allow me to communicate clearly so more and more people can hear and receive the information and so the animals can come through me in a way that's not going to anger or frustrate people. I want to hand this experience to people in a gentle, accessible way."

I had one last question for Kate, one that frequently surfaces when people talk about reincarnation. "Do animals come back as humans?" I asked. "Occasionally," Kate answered. "I've worked with some, but they are a minority." Then Kate turned to Lyris for her response. "Lyris says, 'I really don't have any interest in being a human being. They just have so much stuff to work through.'"

There's something to be said for living a dog's life.

Healer update

Kate Solisti-Mattelon remarried and lives in Northern Colorado. Kate and her husband, Patrice, work together and do healing sessions and nutritional counseling.

They self-published "Balanced Animal Handbook," which covers nutrition, use of flower remedies, training tips, animal communication and spirituality. Their second book, "The Holistic Animal Handbook," is a simple, hands-on guidebook for animal nutrition, health and communication.

Contact information

Kate Solisti-Mattelon
4247 Prado Drive
Boulder, CO 80303
(303) 499-9317
email: solmat@earthlink.net
website: http://home.earthlink.net/~solmat/

Red Levesque & Rachel Blackmer
Animal Healers

We facilitate healing between
animals and humans. But more,
we have the distinct pleasure
of being able to be there when
that door cracks open just a little
bit and that person starts out on
their journey.

It was springtime in the Rockies. Rachel Blackmer, Red Levesque and I sat around the kitchen table in their cozy mountain cabin 10 minutes outside of Conifer, Colorado. Susan Belsky sat off to the side, letting Rachel and Red do the talking.

Lodged against the mountainside and surrounded by long-standing pines and aspen, the rustic cabin is temporary home for these three wholesome, self-sufficient women and their five horses, five dogs and seven cats. The three call themselves Indigo Quill Healing Arts, Integrated Health for Animals. Together they offer a holistic approach to animal health care, primarily through acupuncture, Reiki and classical homeopathy.

Since their clients don't have easy access to their back-roads location, Rachel and Red maintain a mobile practice that takes them throughout Denver's foothills and outlying areas. They treat horses, dogs, cats, birds and reptiles. Until recently, Susan worked at a conventional veterinary hospital. (She's expecting a baby any day now.) The trio's dream is to create a holistic healing center for animals and humans in the Conifer area where they can practice, teach, offer various healing arts and have an outdoor school for classes ranging from animal husbandry to animal spirituality.

Rachel, Red and Susan aren't blood sisters but soul sisters – and highly spirited ones at that – who share the same vision and mission to re-educate humanity so it can live in harmony and balance with nature. All three grew up with horses as a favorite pastime. Their roots are on the East Coast but all call Colorado their home. As Rachel and Red talked about their journeys, their passions and their success stories, they wove a colorful tale of women, horses, dolphins and fire.

Red, who is named for her red hair and rosy complexion, gained notoriety in the late 1970s as the first documented woman farrier in New England. She attended a horseshoeing school in Nebraska after high school then returned to her home state of Connecticut where she operated her own business for four years. During that time she spoke to women's groups, usually intending to talk about how she used a feminine, more gentle and intuitive approach to working with animals rather than one of "brute strength and brawniness." But that was not what the women's groups wanted to hear.

"It was a real awakening process for me," Red said, "because I got into horseshoeing not because it was a male profession and I wanted to prove something, but because I always had this love of horses. It was the thing I could find to do that didn't take tens of thousands of dollars to set up a business. I didn't want to go on to vet school, and you need to have a name for yourself to do horse training. I liked working with my hands so I did horseshoeing instead. I was really the minority."

Connecticut's rural areas were shrinking, and Red longed for wide, open spaces across which she could gallop. So she moved to Colorado in 1980 and fell in love with the paradise she found. She lived in a secluded, wild area in the mountains and began horseshoeing. She also managed a breeding farm for fox-trotting horses, where she tapped into a network of people interested in the spiritual aspect of animals. Red also began looking at the spiritual nature of her own life, and on a dare from one of her clients, took a weekend course on the Tellington Jones Equine Awareness Movement from Linda Tellington Jones of Santa Fe, New Mexico.

Tellington Touch, as it is now called, is a bodywork technique that integrates mind and body by repatterning the animals' neural pathways, ultimately changing behavior. Just 15 minutes into the class, Red said she was hooked and knew that this was going to be her life's work. She signed up for a week-long training seminar and began to use Tellington Touch while shoeing horses and managing horses at a wild horse adoption center in Bailey. "I used her work on these wild horses with amazing results. I was able to put shoes on them and handle them without having them tied or restrained in any way, and the animals were different – they really changed. So, I became really excited about the work and, over the course of the next four years, took nine or 10 week-long trainings with Linda. I became a team trainer and decided to let go of the horseshoeing."

Then Red met Susan. Susan's employer at a horse farm in Vermont had flown Susan to Boulder to take a class in Tellington Touch, a class that Red was student teaching. Red and Susan discovered the commonalities of their lives. They both had spent time in Connecticut and Colorado and had mutual friends and clients, but they never had met. Susan's employer offered Red a job at the Vermont horse farm, and Red returned to the East Coast with her horses in tow.

The two women soon formed New England Equine Re-Education Associates, and for three years traveled up and down the Eastern Seaboard teaching Tellington Touch to a wide variety of clients. Additional travel came through their association with the National Mounted Police School, where they taught mounted police about "the other aspects – the human side – of their vehicle," Red said.

Susan returned to Vermont and began working as a technician at a veterinary hospital. Red was road weary – "You can't get good vegetarian meals anywhere" – and followed Susan to begin a new career as a vet technician where Susan worked. The two used Tellington Touch with great success on dogs and cats, only to discover that Tellington Jones had just expanded her work to include zoo animals, dogs and cats.

Then along came Rachel. Fresh out of veterinary school in Massachusetts, Rachel took a job at the rural vet hospital where Red and Susan worked. "I'm the pup-ette," Rachel said about being six years younger than Red and Susan. The three formed a relationship within the first week of Rachel's arrival. "We were such a team," Rachel continued. "I think that it was all meant to happen that way. The three of us would work together with respect for the animals, respect for the owners. We loved what we were doing, and that mattered more than anything. It was about compassion, holding the animal and letting them know it was going to be OK instead of just 'doing' to them. I think our alternative medicine started right there, using the drugs, using all the standard procedures, but in a different way. It was very cool.

"There were times when we would stay at the clinic overnight and sleep on the floor when an animal was really sick because they needed someone there. Or there were times when we'd send animals home with owners, when our boss might have disagreed, because it was the only way they would have survived. And there were times when animals died that got everything that they needed medically, but were missing something emotionally."

This unconventional approach to working with animals triggered Rachel's need to return to the spirit-based world she had known as a child but lost touch with during her years of higher education. She grew up in a family that met their health needs through chiropractic and homeopathy, so after about six months into the practice Rachel realized "it just wasn't right." She began studying acupuncture through the International Veterinary Acupuncture Society; she and Red started reading books about spirituality and herbology. The two quit their jobs at the clinic and formed their first mobile practice, supplementing their income with horseshoeing. Nine months later in the fall of 1992, after Susan completed horseshoeing school, the three women moved to Colorado.

Horseshoeing once again provided income for Red and Rachel, enabling them to build a large clientele while they continued to study alternative healing. "Because we were two women shoeing and because of the way we handled horses, it was a special kind of person who wanted us to come to work for them," Rachel said. "Within a year, we built up a clientele of about 200 or 300 horses. Many of the people who owned those horses were really interested in a more esoterical approach, so that when we began doing more and more of the alternatives, our horseshoeing clients became alternative medicine clients as well. It was a great transition."

Rachel began studying homeopathy in 1994, and her life changed. "I fell in love with homeopathy, absolutely fell in love with it. I still did some acupuncture; still did some herbs, color therapy and Bach flower remedies. But homeopathy was my love. I've really had a lot of wonderful successes with homeopathy. So that became my fire. Red's was something else. Then the household got caught up in Red's fire."

Red's fire was Reiki, a gentle touch therapy that balances the body's energy systems. With her body feeling the wear and tear of nearly 20 years of horseshoeing, Red had just asked the Universe "to give her something else," Rachel said. A day or so later a friend told Red about a Reiki class. Red took the class, came home and was "obnoxious," Rachel recalled.

"I was not obnoxious," Red quipped.

"Yes, you were," Rachel said with a laugh. "Red was adamant that Susan and I had to take Reiki 'cause it's so wonderful." More than a year later, Red earned the title of Traditional Reiki Master. (She's come a long way since her first classes in Tellington Touch when her classmates jokingly referred to energy as the "E-word" because Red couldn't believe something existed unless she could see or touch it.) Rachel currently is apprenticing with Red to become a Reiki Master, and Susan is a Reiki practitioner. The three have done many Reiki healings on animals and humans, solo and together. They are teaching Reiki for animals as well as for humans, using stuffed animals at first to teach the technique.

"Nobody else is doing Reiki with animals, at least not as a business," Rachel said. "I think if we could do just Reiki and homeopathy we'd be happy, but it's too esoteric for people. Most people can deal with acupuncture, so we'll do acupuncture on animals and often do Reiki at the same time. It's surprising the number of people who notice that you still have your hands on the dog. Then they want to know what you're doing, and they're really interested. We've used it with people who are going through a grieving process with an animal dying. It's just a wonderful modality."

"Look at the goosebumps on your arms," Red laughed, gesturing at Rachel.

"I get excited," Rachel said.

And they have a lot to be excited about. Individually and collectively they have much to offer and are beginning to integrate other talents and interests, such as Red's flair for writing and Rachel's love of illustration. Rachel illustrated a Reiki manual that Red wrote for her master project and that they have been using for their animal Reiki workshops. "It's a compilation of Reiki, Linda Tellington Jones' work, plus the stuff that we learned collectively in our 20 or 30 years' experience in working with animals," Red said. "We did another manual that is advanced work that includes the philosophy of the New World approach to animals. We deal with animal communication, nutrition, holistic healing and health; making the animal a participant and understanding the heart-to-heart connection between man and animals."

The three women often work with animal communicator Kate Solisti of Santa Fe when they need assistance healing an animal. Kate once communicated for Elmo the turtle what it was like to receive Reiki. Red recalled: "He said, 'It's like when I get up on a rock in the sun and a cloud comes by and blocks the sun, then the cloud moves and the sun comes out again.' He is a wise turtle. He was dying, so for him it was like the sun coming out again."

"We use his little description of Reiki in every class we teach," Rachel added.

Indigo Quill also organizes a monthly Reiki circle that honors a particular creature, and is compiling a booklet that includes each creature's spiritual teachings and channeled messages. This extends from the women's personal beliefs based on Native American spirituality. Indigo Quill also is beginning to co-sponsor trips – "they're really Reiki extravaganzas," Rachel said – to Isla

Mujeres (Isle of the Women) in Mexico to swim with dolphins.

"We went down in November 1995 and swam with the dolphins and it was a pivotal experience," Red said. "Dolphins are major healers and do an attunement on people like you would do an attunement on someone in a Reiki class. They move your energy, and you feel it everywhere. It changes your life. We bring in dolphin energy now whenever we do healings."

"The experience will lead people further along their path," Rachel continued. "It will happen for us, too. Every time we teach a class, every time we talk to people."

"That's the most exciting part about what we do," Red continued. "You open the door just a crack and then you stand back and the person makes all these discoveries. Yes, we have these practices, and we facilitate healing between animals and humans. But more, we have the distinct pleasure of being there when that door cracks open just a little bit and that person starts out on their journey."

Their speaking engagements have expanded to include groups of holistic veterinarians, and recently spawned a Reiki class for a group of vet students at Colorado State University. "The web is growing and growing," Red said. "Who knows where it's going to go."

"We just want people to know that there's more out there than a symptom and a drug," Rachel said. "That there is a holistic approach, not just for humans, but for animals, that involves the body, the mind, the emotions and spirituality, for all of us, whether we're four-legged, two-legged, slithering or winged. People can help their animal, they can help themselves."

Red concluded: "It's that empowerment thing that's so important – drawing people back into their energy and the realization of the oneness of everything. We have to re-educate humanity, to bring us back home, to make humanity's connection with the natural kingdom easier. There's a trickle there now, but my mission is to open it up so it becomes a torrent."

Healer update

Red Levesque, Rachel Blackmer and Susan Belsky no longer work together as Indigo Quill Healing Arts.

Red changed her name to Eryn Wolfwaler and formed a new healing practice, Lightfoot Unlimited. Eryn and new partner, Vidya, use holistic methods to bring horses back to nature. These include removing metal shoes and trimming hoofs.

Rachel returned to the East Coast in 1999 where she directs the Humane Society of the United States – Cape Wildlife Center in Cape Cod, Massachusetts.

Susan is raising her son and is living on a ranch in the Conifer, Colorado area.

Contact information

Eryn Wolfwalker
Lightfoot Unlimited
P.O. Box 845
Conifer, CO 80433
(303) 838-7698

GLOSSARY

ACUPUNCTURE ~ An ancient Chinese medical practice that treats acute and chronic illnesses by inserting fine needles into the skin at vital points along meridians or energy pathways. Acupuncture stimulates the flow of energy through the meridians and helps to restore balance to low- or over-functioning organs.

ALLOPATHY ~ The Western method of treating disease with remedies to induce conditions or symptoms different from those accompanying the disease.

APOTHECARY ~ One who makes herbal medicines.

AURA ~ The energy or electromagnetic field that surrounds and penetrates the physical body. The aura extends 2 to 3 feet from the body and comprises seven different layers or levels in which all emotions, thoughts, memories and behaviors can be found. The aura is in constant motion, reacting to input from the environment and to changes in thoughts and feelings. All life forms have auras.

AYURVEDA ~ Ayurveda, which originated in ancient India, is a spiritually based, holistic approach to achieving and maintaining well-being through diet and lifestyle. It is a system of healing based on the five element theory.

BLOCK or BLOCKAGE ~ Blocks or energy blocks are an absence of light, areas that are clogged with stagnant energy. Blocks originate in the aura or energy field as distorted beliefs and thoughts, and as emotions like fear or worry, then work their way into the physical body.

They can be experienced as muscular tightness caused by unconscious holding patterns, such as elevating the shoulders up towards the ears or clenching teeth, or they can be experienced in organs and systems with symptoms ranging from constipation and poor circulation to ulcers and tumors.

BODY-MIND CENTERING ~ An experiential study of anatomical, physiological and developmental principles that uses movement, touch, sound and guided imagery. Founded by Bonnie Bainbridge Cohen, Body-Mind Centering uses movement re-education and hands-on repatterning to change limiting movement patterns and enhance perceptual-motor development.

CHAKRAS ~ There are seven major chakras or energy centers located in the physical body that govern a person's physical, emotional, mental and spiritual well-being. Chakras are located along the spine on the front and back of the body and are perceived as vortexes funneling up from the body into the aura. The first or root chakra is located at the base of the spine; the seventh or crown chakra is located at the top of the head and is said to look like a thousand-petaled lotus.

CHIROPRACTIC ~ The practice of treating imbalances in the body by manipulating the bones of the spine as well as the joints. Holistic chiropractic supports structural alignments with diet, supplements, herbs and energy therapies like Reiki and acupuncture.

CLAIRVOYANCE ~ Clairvoyance is the ability to see, hear, smell, taste and touch things beyond the normal range of human perception. It is the ability to see or perceive a picture in the mind without using normal vision.

CO-CREATE ~ Working cooperatively with others and with one's innate spiritual power in a conscious and non-judgmental way for the purpose of personal and collective growth and development.

CRANIOSACRAL THERAPY ~ CranioSacral Therapy balances the flow of cerebrospinal fluid in the brain and spinal cord through light pressure.

CURANDERA ~A traditional Hispanic woman healer.

CURANDERISMO ~ The Hispanic art of healing.
Curanderismo is a system of folk medicine which is holistic and nature-based, and embraces the use of herbs, bodywork, rituals and prayer.

DEVELOPMENTAL MOVEMENT ~ Developmental movement, one aspect of Body-Mind Centering, explores the movement patterns that are the foundation of efficient adult movement. Movement repatterning helps clients, especially children who suffer birth trauma and brain injury, experience pieces of the movement sequence they missed in their developmental process.

DIMENSIONS ~ Other planes or levels of existence; realities above or beyond what we perceive with the five senses.

DOSHA ~ An Ayurvedic term used to describe a person's basic constitution or body type. The five elements recognized in Eastern practices - earth, air, fire, water and ether or space - combine to create the three doshas: Vata, Pitta, Kapha.

DOULAS ~ The Ayurvedic word for mother helpers, women who provide postpartum care for mothers. Doulas cook, clean house, do child care and mother-baby massage for up to six weeks after the baby's birth.

EARTH MEDICINE ~ A healing practice that originated with nature-based religions and uses the elements - earth, air, fire, water - and other parts of nature to create change or restore balance and harmony. Earth medicine acknowledges that Earth and its creatures carry wisdoms and qualities that enhance healing and contribute to good health.

ENERGY ~ The life-giving force that moves throughout the aura and the physical body; the vital force that exists in all living things and throughout the universe. Eastern practices refer to energy as chi, qi, ki or prana.

ENERGY WORK ~ A variety of therapies performed with hands on the body or in the energy field with the intention of moving energy and releasing blocks to facilitate and support healing. Examples of energy therapies are Polarity and Reiki.

ESSENTIAL OILS ~ The highly concentrated oily substances that are extracted from plants through distillation. Considered the spirit or soul of the plant, essential oils are the most concentrated form of herbal energy used for healing, and contain hormones, vitamins, antibiotics and antiseptics. The oils have healing properties that affect the physical, mental, emotional and spiritual bodies. The art and science of using essential oils to heal is called aromatherapy and dates back to ancient Egypt.

ETHERIC FIELD ~ The first of seven layers of the auric field, the etheric field is associated with the first chakra and the physical functions and sensations of the body. The etheric field extends from 1/4 to 2 inches beyond the pysical body, and its color varies from light blue to gray.

FIELD ~ The space surrounding the body; an invisible, multi-dimensional blueprint that defines who we are. Field transcends time and space.

FLOWER ESSENCES ~ Flower essences are subtle energy medicines that are made by infusing flowers to extract the chemicals that compose their basic character or spirit. Each flower essence has qualities that correspond to human personality traits, emotions, attitudes and life challenges. For example, chamomile and arnica ease shock and emotional distress. Essences restore health by balancing the electrical system and stabilizing the nervous system.

HOLISTIC ~ A healing approach that looks at the whole person - their body, mind, emotions and spirit, their inner and outer environments - when dealing with disease. Holistic practitioners look for and treat the underlying causes of disease with a wide range of natural healing methods. Holistic also refers to lifestyle choices - living in a way that supports the balance of body, mind, emotions and spirit.

HOMEOPATHY ~ A system of medicine that uses natural remedies derived from minute amounts of animal, vegetable and mineral substances. Homeopathy is based on an age-old concept of the law of similars, or "like is cured by like:" minute amounts of a substance will cure symptoms produced by larger amounts of the same substance. Practitioners select a needed remedy by matching the symptoms of the individual to the symptoms induced by the remedy.

KAYAKALPA ~ The Ayurvedic term for body time, a six-week period following childbirth when the mother often experiences expanded consciousness and improved health.

MASSAGE THERAPY ~ The art of using touch to promote health and relaxation. Massage has been used since ancient times to soothe and heal the sick and to relieve pain in muscles and joints. There are many forms of massage therapy, which range from the invigorating to the soothing to those designed to treat specific injuries. Western forms generally use oils applied to the skin; Eastern forms more often are done on a fully clothed client.

MEDITATION ~ The art of contemplation. Meditation is a tool used to expand consciousness to a higher level of awareness. It stills the mind and rejuvenates the body. There are many types of meditation. They include focusing on breath, circulating energy or light throughout the body, or the use of sounds - mantras or chants.

MERIDIANS ~ The pathways or channels that carry energy or qi through the body. They compose an invisible network that nourishes the body and maintains balance. Each meridian corresponds to an organ or system and performs specific functions.

METAPHYSICAL ~ That which deals with anything beyond the physical, the unseen. The philosophy of metaphysics deals with the nature, character and causes of being and knowing.

MIDWIFERY ~ The practice of delivering babies at home or in a clinic setting with the assistance of women experienced in birthing procedures. Midwives provide both pre-and post-natal care in a holistic way.

MULTIDIMENSIONAL ~ The entire spectrum of human energy defined by the aura or energy field.

MUSCLE TESTING ~ Muscle testing or applied kinesiology is a method of allowing the subconscious to respond in yes or no answers by strong or weak muscle responses in the arm or fingers. This type of muscle testing (there are many types) is based on several theories: That truth always strengthens and falsehood weakens or shatters the electromagnetic field; that the body reacts positively or negatively to an object that enters its energy field; that every word or thought has a vibration that will or won't resonate with the energy field. Muscle testing can be used as a tool to tap the body's wisdom for sources of illness and guidelines for healing.

NATUROPATHY ~ A holistic and preventive practice that honors the natural healing power of nature and emphasizes healthy living through a diet of whole foods, fresh air and exercise. A naturopath treats the whole person, focusing on the cause of illness rather than the treatment of symptoms. Naturopaths often use a variety of healing methods including nutritional counseling, herbology, acupuncture, homeopathy and energy work.

NUMEROLOGY ~ Numerology is the science of numbers and, like the tarot, is a tool for reading a person's energy and offering insights into his or her life.

PAGANISM ~ An ancient, nature-oriented religion that recognizes many gods and honors Mother Earth, her cycles and our relationships to them. Rituals are an important part of Paganism.

PROCESSING ~ The way in which a person synthesizes insights and information gained through body-mind therapies.

PSYCHIC ~ One who is sensitive to supernatural forces.

QI ~ (pronounced chee) The Chinese word for energy. Also spelled chi or ki.

QI GONG ~ An ancient Chinese form of meditation that incorporates mind and breathing exercises. It means energy cultivation. Considered the equivalent of yoga, Qi Gong has many forms. Same as Chi Kung.

REIKI ~ (ray-key) A practice discovered in ancient Tibetan scriptures by Dr. Mikao Usui of Japan and introduced to the West in 1937. This gentle touch therapy uses chi, universal life energy, to balance the body's energy systems and can be used on one's self as well as others.

ROLFING ~ A form of bodywork that uses deep tissue massage to strengthen and realign the body. Realignment is achieved by reshaping the fascia or body stocking that encases muscle, a process that releases physical and emotional trauma stored in body tissue.

SHAMAN ~ A medicine man or woman who uses ancient techniques, intuition and imagination to journey to the world of spirit for information and knowledge. Some of the areas a shaman might specialize in are healing, developing power and prophesying.

SHAMANISM ~ A primitive religion and art that acknowledges and honors the spirit that exists in all living things. Shamanism believes that all life forms are interconnected and that humankind's survival depends on their harmonious relationships.

SHIATSU ~ A Japanese form of bodywork that uses manual pressure along energy pathways or meridians to stimulate and balance energy flow and promote health. Shiatsu means finger pressure, although pressure also is applied with other parts of the hand and the elbows and knees.

TAI CHI or **TAIJI** ~ An ancient Chinese form of movement meditation that historically was linked to the martial arts. Its contemplative postures and movements revitalize as well as produce a sense of serenity and well-being. Tai Chi is considered a healing art.

TAROT ~ A set of cards with numbers and images used in psychic readings to convey information about a person's past, present or future. Tarot cards are useful in finding solutions to dilemmas and analyzing a person's character.

TELEPATHIC ~ One who communicates with other people or creatures without the normal use of the senses.

TINCTURE ~ A concentrated plant preparation. The healing properties of plants are extracted and preserved by soaking fresh or freshly dried herbs in grain alcohol. After two weeks, the mixture is strained and the liquid stored in amber bottles.

TRADITIONAL CHINESE MEDICINE (TCM) ~ Developed in ancient China, Traditional Chinese Medicine is a holistic approach to healing that is based on yin-yang theory. TCM uses information gathered through the five senses to diagnose illness. Tongue and pulse diagnosis are important parts of this process. Treatments include acupuncture, herbs and diet and lifestyle changes.

TRADITIONAL ORIENTAL MEDICINE (TOM) ~ A holistic approach to medicine that incorporates traditional practices from China, Japan and other Asian countries.

TUI-NA ~ (pronounced twee-na) A form of Chinese massage in which the practitioner uses light pressure on acupressure points and joint stretches to stimulate the flow of energy through the meridians.

YIN-YANG ~ Yin-yang is an ancient Chinese system of thought which recognizes that all things have two elements - yin and yang - and that all things are parts of a whole. Yin qualities are cold, passive, dark, inward; yang qualities are hot, active, light and outward. The two elements interact as complementary opposites. Disease results when these elements are out of balance.

YOGA ~ Practiced in India as far back as 6,000 years ago, yoga is a system of movements and postures that incorporates breath. Yoga means union, and its practice joins body, mind and spirit to gain a deeper awareness of self. There are 10 forms of yoga, the most popular being hatha yoga, which stretches and tones the body.

ZEN ~ A Japanese sect of Buddhism that teaches enlightenment by intuition rather than formal study. Sitting meditation, the practice of being in the present moment by recognizing and releasing thoughts and focusing on breath, is an important part of Zen teachings.

BIBLIOGRAPHY

Brennen, Barbara Ann, *"Hands of Light."* Bantam Books, New York, NY, 1988.

Davis, Patricia, *"Aromatherapy An A-Z."* The C.W. Daniel Company Limited, Saffron Walden, Essex, England, 1988.

Gach, Michael Reed, and Marco, Carolyn, *"Acu-Yoga."* Japan Publications, Inc., Tokyo, Japan, and New York, NY, 1981.

Griscom, Chris, *"Ecstasy Is a New Frequency."* Bear & Company, Santa Fe, NM, 1987.

Joy, Dr. W. Brugh, *"Joy's Way."* J.P. Tarcher, Inc., Los Angeles, CA, 1979.

Kaptchuk, Ted J., *"The Web That Has No Weaver."* Congdon & Weed, Inc., New York, NY, 1983.

Lavabre, Marcel F., *"Aromatherapy Workbook."* Healing Arts Press, Rochester, VT, 1990.

Lidell, Lucinda, *"The Book of Massage."* Simon & Schuster Inc., New York, NY, 1984.

Masunaga, Shizuto, and Ohashi, Wataru, *"Zen Shiatsu."* Japan Publications, Tokyo, Japan, and New York, NY, 1977.

Morningstar, Amadea, and Desai, Urmila, *"The Ayurvedic Cookbook."* Lotus Press, Twin Lakes, WI, 1995.

Panos, Dr. Maesimund B., and Heimlich, Jane, *"Homeopathic Medicine at Home."* The Putnam Publishing Group, New York, NY, 1980.

Perrone, Bobette, Stockel, H. Henrietta, and Krueger, Victoria, *"Medicine Women, Curanderas, and Women Doctors."* University of Oklahoma Press, Norman, OK, 1989.

"Rodale's Illustrated Encyclopedia of Herbs." Rodale Press, Emmaus, PA, 1987.

Rosenberg, Jack Lee, Rand, Marjorie L., and Asay, Diane, *"Body, Self & Soul: Sustaining Integration."* Humanics Limited, Atlanta, GA, 1985.

Small, Jacquelyn, *"Awakening in Time."* Bantam Books, New York, NY, 1991.

Stevens, Dr. Jose, and Stevens, Lena S., *"Secrets of Shamanism."* Avon Books, New York, NY, 1988.

Taber, Clarence Wilbur, *"Taber's Cyclopedic Medical Dictionary."* F.A. Davis Company, Philadelphia, PA, 1960.

Toguchi, Masaru, and Warren, Dr. Frank Z., *"Complete Guide to Acupuncture and Acupressure."* Gramercy Publishing Company, New York, NY, 1985.

Wright, Machaelle Small, *"Map: the Co-Creative White Brotherhood Medical Assistance Program."* Perelandra, Ltd., Warrenton, VA, 1980.

Carol Kronwitter is a healer, an artist and a writer. She received a certificate of massage therapy from Boulder College of Massage Therapy in 1989. In October 1997, Carol and three other healers began highly guided work to heal humanity and the planet. Through their sophisticated work and an expanded network of healers, they are raising the consciousness and vibration of all living forms on Earth.

Carol's healing practice includes massage therapy, energy work derived from LaHo-Chi, spiritual counseling and a variety of vibrational therapies. She and her canine friend, Lyris, live in Pueblo, Colorado.